Praise for Chris Erskine's Books

"The worst of times brought out the best of him."
—Peter Mehlman, former "Seinfeld" writer/producer,
author of *#MeAsWell* and *Mandela Was Late*

"Every word, every sentence Chris Erskine writes makes me want to salute him with two fingers of Jameson in shared grief, love, laughter, and life. And now him writing about the plague of our time? Time to toast with the whole bottle."
—Gustavo Arellano, the *Los Angeles Times*, author of *Taco USA*

"If I have to come and hand sell this book to each of you, I'll do it. This book is so funny and so good—and so short and so elegantly published—that you will be thrilled to own it. I tracked the guy down with a fan letter. A+"
— Caitlin Flanagan, contributing editor of *The Atlantic* and former staff writer at *The New Yorker*

"Charming, well written, concise, and to the point. Perfect for anyone who enjoys stories of fatherhood."
— *Library Journal*

"Erskine touches on the joys and fears that come part and parcel with having small, dependent people living in your house, making the personal universal through the feelings evoked within each column."
— *BookNAround*

More Books
by Chris Erskine

Man of the House

Daditude

Surviving Suburbia

Lavender in Your Lemonade

BY CHRIS ERSKINE

A FUNNY AND TOUCHING

COVID DIARY

Lavender in Your Lemonade:
A Funny and Touching COVID Diary

Cover Designed by Siori Kitajima, SF AppWorks LLC
Illustration by Lars Leetaru

Cataloging-in-Publication data for this book is available from the Library of Congress
ISBN-13:
eBook: 978-1-950154-26-5
Paperback: 978-1-950154-25-8

Published by The Sager Group LLC
TheSagerGroup.net

Lavender in Your Lemonade

BY CHRIS ERSKINE

A FUNNY AND TOUCHING COVID DIARY

THE SAGER GROUP

Artifex Te Adiuva

contents

Publisher's Note

Since I moved to California over two decades ago, I have been a subscriber to the *Los Angeles Times*, and it was in those newsprint pages, tossed onto my driveway in the early hours of the morning by a small man driving an El Camino, who appeared to be buried up to his armpits in rolled and plastic-bagged newspapers, where I first encountered Chris Erskine's work, especially his columns about family life.

Writing a regular column is incredibly difficult. First, it is a privilege given to only a few, so you have to be good; a zillion other writers are standing in line behind you, eager for their chance. Once you get the nod, the deadlines keep rolling, rolling, rolling, and each time you have to find a way to invent anew the same general topic. Writing a regular column about family life, that most universal condition of humankind, seems even more daunting. Everyone has a family. Everyone thinks their own family is cute or madcap or bat-turd crazy, or maybe tragic and dark, equally newsworthy on another scale. In any case, what Erskine has published over the past 30 years at the *Times* (25 as a columnist) has been consistently worthy of publication in a legacy publication that currently boasts (according to the *L.A. Times* web page) a combined print and online local weekly audience of 4.6 million.

Erskine is a both a newsman and a wordsmith, one of the last of the old school. His finely chiseled prose reflects this combination and harkens to great newspaper columnists of the past, like Mike Royko and Erma Bombeck, drawing simple truths from the infinite complexities of the human condition, 800 words at a time.

As a younger man, Erskine's eye for telling detail, along with his gift for coinage and turns of phrase, made his work a delightful read. Later, as he weathered the storms of tragedy and heartbreak that befall all of us, his voice and point of view took on the beauty and bittersweetness of an Irish tenor.

Now comes *Lavender in Your Lemonade: A Funny and Touching COVID Diary*, in which he tackles the New Normal with his chronical of daily life under the frustrating, terrifying, and sometimes antic strictures of a worldwide pandemic.

No, it's not funny. And yet somehow, in Erskine's hands, it is.

Or at least it feels more tolerable.

—Mike Sager

FOREWORD

The Worst of Times Brought out the Best of Him

As someone who occasionally and painstakingly squeezed out op-ed columns for the *Los Angeles Times*, I had a no-choice mission to contact Chris Erskine.

His output in the paper was so prolific, I just had to prove that this smiley, mustache-and-glasses guy wasn't acting alone. My guess was he had a secret operation going on, like James Patterson or Andy Warhol—a whole team of underlings who listen to his every one-liner and column idea and churn out product under the name of their Svengali. After all, without the benefit of a secret factory, it was impossible to believe that one, two-legged human being could write so many absorbing, funny, and wistfully brilliant columns by himself.

Contacting him nearly amounted to investigative reporting: What's the truth about this guy?

As it turned out, the truth about this guy was... truth.

Chris is a newspaperman. For those unfamiliar with that term, he is the kind of reporter who dredges up truth out of sheer powers of observation, curiosity, instinct and yes, habit. He is the kind of throw-back who probably refers to himself as an "ink-stained wretch." He's Bob Woodward with a sense of humor.

Unlike most great reporters, Chris is insanely versatile. At the *Times*, he wrote about sports, family, restaurants, total strangers he met by chance ... there was seemingly no observation that went unnoticed, no subject field he couldn't write about.

In a city where it feels as if everyone is a transplant who just came here and meekly tried to fit in, Chris was also an alien to Los Angeles. But he didn't submit to just fitting in. He didn't float above the facts of his adopted LA. He took the time to learn everything about this mind-blowing city and explain it for the rest of us. His *Times* columns have been eyes and ears for the deaf and blind ... you know, all the rest of us who live here.

In 2009 (I think) we finally had lunch near the beautiful, now depressingly shuttered, LA Times building. The restaurant was a joint, the kind of busy greasy spoon we both loved. We ate cholesterol burgers, saturated fat fries and joked about how our lunch should come with a free angioplasty.

We talked sports, dished about newspaper people we did (and didn't) have in common. I had the thought that I was probably among 10,000 people who'd met Chris and felt like I'd known him my whole life. Then again, when someone writes so effortlessly and insightfully about the little quirks of life we all experience, you expect that person to be pretty nailed down to the planet Earth.

We've had several lunches since, most recently in Santa Monica, during which Chris leaked the information that he'd be done at the *Times* soon. He saw the demise of newspapers way before most and held on as long as he could. He held on long enough to use his columns to describe the worst year of his life. I remember tearing open the paper for those columns and simultaneously wanting to read and to look away. From column to column, you never knew whether you'd wind up laughing or crying by the end. No small feat.

The worst of times brought out the best of him.

Now, the worst of times has gone global and The *Times* doesn't have Chris Erskine to interpret it all for us.

In a word, that sucks.

But then again, it's not like he owes us anything.

And it's not like he's stopped writing...

—Peter Mehlman

The Lockdown Begins

I rish as a boiled carrot, I always celebrate Patrick's Day in my usual way, hollering Yeats's "The Wild Swans at Cole" on street corners and small social gatherings of doctors and deadbeats.

I have looked upon those brilliant creatures,
And now my heart is sore ...

The bell-beat of their wings above my head,
Trod with a lighter tread.

In my own peculiar way, I am keeping the Irish Literary Revival alive. I'm also testing my lungs for all the obvious things.

My theory is that if you can bellow Yeats at full throat, you're probably just fine. The CDC has yet to weigh in on this. But I've appointed myself the surgeon general of our little cul-de-sac, so it's not like I'm without medical pedigree.

What a week, right?

I'd like to assure you that everything is going to be all right, which it is, though I've been wrong before. I thought computers were just a phase and that, by now, Bill Murray or George Will would be elected president. Wrong and wrong.

Now I think that, come the warming months, this virus will lose its spirit, and that by autumn there'll be a shot for it. I'm not sitting idle though, waiting for others to take action. I've developed my own answer to COVID-19.

A cocktail called the Quarantini.

It started when they canceled Coachella, leaving me bereft and in need of a reason to go on with life. I tend to prefer Stagecoach, but they canceled that too. In two days, they canceled pretty much everything. By Wednesday, they'd called off Christmas.

The last public event I attended was a bookstore bash in Manhattan Beach, a festive evening that propelled me through the weekend. Missing from our lives right now are twinkly eyes and leprechaun smirks. And double-ply, of course.

My kid sister happened to be back in town through all this, a blessing in disguise, for she is a twinkly soul, more Irish than I am. She was here to tend to her daughter, Amy, who was having her ACL renovated after a jumpy ski run went wonky.

So there we were, sitting around playing Catan, the hot new board game, and making giant vats of chili. It wasn't so bad, for I like having people around, even family.

We put a fire in the fireplace. It rained. We threw on another log. The boy made guacamole. The chili turned out well, even though I'd bought some off-brand beans, the only ones left on the shelf. But I could make decent chili from woodchips. To spice it up, I use thumbtacks and gunpowder (a tip I picked up from a Texan).

Then Amy's boyfriend came into town. It's a very nice time to visit L.A., everything in a state of turmoil, the hospitals all full.

I like the guy, low-key and capable, much like me. Then a mini-crisis: Another niece was stuck in Spain, where she plays soccer for a living. If you think that none of this sounds normal, welcome to our family. (Or any family.)

But my niece managed to catch a plane to the States, and my sister advised her to come to the family compound here in California. After all, he had, like, seven rolls of TP left, and this board game Catan.

She told her daughter that Uncle Chris (that's me) bought too much corned beef and was running around screaming Yeats, as though caroling.

"It'll be fun!" my sister said.

"We have plenty!" I lied.

"I'll be there!" my niece lied back.

So everyone was lying, which is pretty normal for families like ours.

Not sure where we stand right now. Are more people coming? Will the TP and vermouth hold out? Will this new craft cocktail, the Quarantini, be a significant hit?

My clever, mad-hatted colleague Patt Morrison named it, but the recipe is mine: two parts vodka, a whisper of vermouth, a hint of decongestant (for color) — shaken with ice, then served in a chilled martini glass with a couple of cough drops ... Ker plunk, Ker plunk. Cheers!

"Your commitment and compassion are both beyond extraordinary," one friend noted.

Hey, you don't become a cul-de-sac surgeon general for nothing.

My buddy Jeff suggested that a Quarantini is merely a regular martini, except that you drink it at home alone, as per a quarantine.

That just seemed sad. I won't be sad. I'll be my ebullient Irish self, as I try to get a grip on this Catan, which seems kind of complicated. And COVID-19, which seems even worse.

Maybe I should write. Another friend reminded us that when Shakespeare was quarantined, he wrote King Lear.

What a hoot that was. Maybe I could update that, add some laughs? I think Lear's daughters were involved, right? Daughters are good. Daughters are funny. Me, I've never had any issues with daughters.

I'll mix them up some Quarantinis. One day soon, I'll make you one too.

Hang in there, my friend.

Loving
My Captors

ostage Day 10:

The situation here remains very tense. As feared, the chicken I baked last night turned out to be the Road Runner from the classic cartoon, stringy and almost entirely without breast meat, a situation I've run into before. When I carved it, it emitted this tiny "Beep-Beep," as if mocking me. It was all bones and sass.

All I could think of was that poor Wile E. Coyote, who devoted his life to chasing down this jittery idiot ... this Audrey Hepburn creature. Imagine the disappointment, had he ever caught the Road Runner. All that TNT wasted. When you think about it, it's all very chase-my-demons Melville.

Thing is, I don't trust my captors, even as I fall deeper in love with them, a la Patty Hearst. They pass the long evenings playing Scrabble for money and mixing up different flavors of White Claw just for fun, the way millennials will.

They huddle over their phones and giggle at things I do not understand. They watch "That '70s Show," as if anything with Ashton Kutcher could ever be any good.

Indeed, it was a weird weekend. No church. No games going on in the background on TV. Really not sure how much more I can take of this. Beep-Beep! Beep-Beep!

One captor, my own son, joked at dinner last night that when the ramen runs out, we'll have to make soup of the weakest member of the tribe, then winked at me. Even the dog smirked a little and did a little happy dance. I've devoted my life to that wolf-dog, and now she's sizing me up for soup.

My escape plan is this: Yesterday, I discovered that Lou Malnati's is still delivering deep-dish Chicago pizza. I plan to purchase two of them. Everyone passes out after deep-dish pizza, everyone, even wolves; it's the worst kind of coma. At which point I will run out through the front door to freedom.

But where will I go? All the bars are closed. The gyms. The movie theaters. The jazz joints. I imagine encountering 100 other fathers, all fleeing the house at the same time, standing around looking at each other. It'll be just like Back-to-School Night at the high school.

"Now what?" someone will ask.

"I've got booze in the basement," I'll say. "Let's go!"

Something else while I have you: Lou Malnati's is also shipping Door County cherry pie, with tart cherries from Hyline Orchards in Fish Creek, Wisconsin.

Dear gawd, just when you think you can't go on another day — without sports, without hugs and handshakes and fresh dairy — you run across pizza and cherry pie.

Life goes on.

I Have
Eggs!

In our last episode, we were trying to figure out how Bradley Cooper got to be California's governor, and why he closed the beaches and then ordered Navy hospital ships off the coast when no one could reach them except maybe surfers and other deadbeats who all look exactly like Bradley Cooper.

Suspicious, right? Good-looking people are always looking out for one another, as if they need the extra help.

Me, all I need is some TP and a half-bottle of Schlitz, and I am totally happy.

This whole situation has given me so much wisdom and perspective. It's made me grow up a whole lot.

Yet people still ask: "Are you a hostage or just a dad stuck at home?" and I answer: "What's the difference? Send the cops!"

Tie a yellow ribbon around an old oak tree. Pour another shot. The hostages will be home soon. Hope is everywhere, and when we run out of that, we have the cut-rate drugstore tequila from the fall tailgate season to fall back on. We'll make soup!

Point is: No one should ever just quit.

Don't hate me, but yesterday, we found eggs and toilet paper about a mile from the house. It was a minor miracle, and I almost kissed the clerk, before realizing that might actually kill her. Who knows what kind of viruses I carry these days, plus I'm a really horrible kisser. "Like a carwash ... slurp, slurp," my wife, Posh, used to say.

The eggs and the TP boosted the morale of my captors, because Easter isn't such a long way off, and all we had were plastic eggs. Can you imagine Easter without eggs?

It bought me another day with these hooligans. And the TP! It was like we'd conquered Rome or something.

My niece-captor was on a big, important conference call for work when I got home.

"I have eggs!" I yelled, carrying the tray into camera range.

That's the state of American business right now.

Then I shared my little secret with another hostage parent, after swearing her to secrecy.

"I have big news, but you can't tell anyone, OK?" I texted. "Not nobody."

"I'm pregnant?"

"Bigger than that," I said, and told her about the toilet paper and the eggs.

She didn't seem all that impressed. In fact, she tied to out-impress me with a tip on a Korean market that stocked everything, including eggs and TP and about 400 kinds of kimchi.

That gives you a little insight into the kind of twisted community we live in. No one is happy for anyone else, we just try to out-impress each other, especially the Chardonnay Moms who run the place.

"Plus, you're pregnant," I told her, just so she didn't get too comfortable.

You know how you stop unwanted pregnancies? Quit shaving your legs and give your husband a really bad haircut. You won't want to go near each other.

I know I joke a lot, but I am seriously worried about you and want you to know that.

This will all be over soon, possibly even in our lifetimes. We will look back and laugh at how much we grew to hate our own families, the greatest things in our lives.

The other night, I overheard this exchange:

"I really hate you," one said.

"I hate you more," one answered.

Like that, back and forth for about an hour.

One friend, her name is Muffie (no, really), says some doctor on TV said that in difficult times like these, we should focus on finding inner peace. And to achieve this, we should always finish things we start, which will bring more calm to our lives.

Makes sense, right?

So Muffie looked through her house to find things she hadn't finished. She started by finishing off a bottle of Merlot, then a bottle of Chardonnay, then the remainder of the Valium and a big whoppin' double-box of dark chocolates.

"I feel feckin fablus rite now," she texted later.

Keep smiling, my friends.

The Charmin Virus

America seems to have an endless supply of liquor and ammo — same thing? Funny the things that soothe us. Lots of folks fostering puppies and kittens to pass the time and take their minds off the health crisis.

In our house, they're fostering me.

We're in Day *!@*&%$&%#&^$ of this worldwide Charmin Virus. If I don't grill some meat soon, I may go really bonkers. Of the things that soothe us, firing up the grill may be the very best.

Here's what you need to know about me: Grilled beef is my love language; Vodka is my spirit animal; I'm a lousy kisser; I find Jack Black, like, really annoying.

I don't like Trader Joe's either. Shocking, I know. I'm probably the only person in America that doesn't worship Trader Joe's and all those rice cakes and roasted pepper sauces.

I like the people who work there — I trust them more than my doctor. They are smart and eager, and were I to start a village from scratch, I'd fill it with Trader Joe's employees, that's how much I like them.

I also hate *The New Yorker*, except for their movie critic, the great Anthony Lane.

What do I like? Well, vodka, as I said, and I like crooked old mailboxes at the end of country lanes, the way they all lean into each other like old pals. I like the way snow piles on them at Christmas.

I like Brahms and old Rusty Springfield albums. I like Utah.

I even like the TSA. No, I'm serious. I get patted down by the TSA every single time. I don't know if it's the mercury in my system from too much sushi, or the aluminum piping that gives shape to my overpriced jeans, but TSA staffers pull me aside to frisk me every time I go through the detector.

AND I LIKE IT!

Trust me, I always overtip. When I leave the house for the airport, my last thought is: Do I have enough singles for folks at the TSA?

Ah, remember the silly the things we used to complain about? Remember when we were all up in arms over paper straws, or single-use baggies, or that entitled mom on the Peloton bike? Or the cheatin', lyin' Astros?

Okay, we're still pretty pissed about the Astros.

Point is, milder spring mornings are upon us and better times lie ahead. Here in California, the calla lilies are starting to bloom, jutting up out of our chocolate-brown gardens like pretty blond knives. Of course, we can't see them, because the governor has forced us inside at gunpoint, probably the right thing. Still, it's suffocating.

But we're all going through this together, and it will be our lifelong bond. It will be the low bar by which we judge future troubles. We will tell the grandkids about it and use it as a topic when we meet strangers on planes in 20 years.

No country rebounds like America. We are the world's comeback kids.

I feel very bad for the students who are missing sports seasons and proms. But as someone pointed out, in the 1960s, boys missed proms because they were being sent off to die in a war.

This is war of a different sort. But our kids are home. And some sort of Easter is just down the lane.

Wedding Postponed

L et's recap a wonderful week:

I lack enthusiasm for Trader Joe's. There, I've said it twice now, and at least one person agrees with me, though I hear good things about the spatchcock chicken and the goat cheese rolled in blueberries. Honestly, sometimes TJ's seems a parody of itself.

As do I.

Other things we learned on one of the longest weeks of our lives:

- I'm a seriously lousy kisser.
- The Chardonnay Moms run our little suburb, but there is also a splinter guerilla group of Tequila Moms. Watch out for them. Their sweaters are a little tighter. They scowl a lot and leave weaker people in their wake, especially husbands.
- Our pretty boy governor once made a movie with Lady Gaga.
- Facebook pals, hearing of my plight, keep offering to drop off booze (the answer is yes ... always yes. Please leave it on the porch next to the firewood and the extra ammo).
- My Twitter friend Gigi reports that she's growing out her beard.

- In my house, there is me and my four armed captors: my son, my demented pet wolf, my niece and her boyfriend, Danny. Of all of them, my own son scares me the most.

He's got his learner's permit, and we spend long afternoons driving on empty roads so that he can accumulate wisdom and driving hours. They have closed the DMVs, and I am thinking of letting him drive alone, illegally, because I think he is qualified and that the world has better things to worry about.

But where would he go? As it is, we drive in big sweeping loops around the Rose Bowl, admiring the crazy March mushroom clouds. It is pretty much the highlight of my day.

Then there's the wolf. Her name is White Fang, and she was born in a whiskey barrel in an old mining camp somewhere in the Sierra Nevada. Posh won her in a poker game. As you might expect, she's got a lot of lousy habits. For example, she smokes.

She also thinks that we are married.

When I kneel down to futz with something — the Wi-Fi, a sock drawer — White Fang will rest her chin on the back of my ankle. Sometimes, I will stall a little just to let her have her moment. Of all my captors, I like her the most. In fact, I love her. It's a serious case of the Stockholm Syndrome. I'd always thought the Stockholm Syndrome was when you craved a lot of reindeer meat and pickled herring. Apparently, it's a little more complicated than that, though I do crave pickled herring and don't trust anyone who doesn't.

The other night, my captors forced me to watch a reality TV show called "Love Is Blind." It involved a bunch of young singles who chose whom to marry based on blind conversations, not appearances. In fact, they had no idea what their prospective mates looked like.

That's an idealized view of lust and human relationships. As you'd suspect, when the contestants all got together, they were drawn to the pretty faces they didn't pick. Drama ensued. And they guzzled a lot of wine — way too much. Though I don't judge.

For two weeks, I have been drinking rum out of one of Posh's old cowboy boots. At this point, I can almost see the back of the liquor cabinet. In a few days, I'll be drinking Bailey's Irish Cream mixed with motor oil. Out of the same old cowboy boot.

Should I be worried?

No, bigger things are upon us. My lovely and patient older daughter, whom I adore more than life itself, had to push back her April wedding.

I feel for the many prospective brides going through all this as we head into wedding season. And, more so, the friends who have sick relatives in Boston and Madrid that they cannot visit.

For every little smile, every funny TikTok video, there are serious and troubling developments.

My buddy Jay confesses to, just before sleep, doing a couple of test swallows and wondering: "Is that a sore throat?"

Just before sleep, let's not fret more than we have to. The end of this week seemed better than the start. The stores are stocked, the stock markets seem steadier.

Soon, weddings will be back. So, too, will our amazing and blessed lives.

Have a weekend. You earned it.

Roots Are showing

At some point, men will need haircuts, and the nail salons will be forced to reopen, or this thing could get really serious. As it is, a lot of husbands are discovering that their wives have been coloring their hair. Once relationship secrets like that start spilling out, where does it end?

Turns out the Chardonnay Moms in our little town require a bit of maintenance. The husbands require almost zero. Once in a while, you splash them with Lysol.

"OK, dear, turn around," the wives say, and blast them with the garden hose.

Remember "Dry January," when all the women quit drinking? Apparently that turned into "Chardonnay March," when everybody had a toot or two at lunch, even the pets.

Dear Lord, what will April bring?

It has also come to my attention that our little suburb now also has Tequila Moms, even more thirsty/bold/alluring than the Chardonnay Moms. It's like gang warfare. And the kids are stuck at home with them. Yikes.

We live now in a world of our own small, comforting habits. Everyone is coping differently. My bored son and I pass long days practicing his driving. We drive round and round in giant loops, admiring the mushroom clouds of spring.

For a new driver, he's doing very well, though I have to remind him that Audis and other luxe sedans always have the right of way, at least here in California.

And he doesn't quite get stop signs. Once, he actually came to a full stop, and the driver behind him honked.

"See?" I told him. "You're just supposed to pause a little."

"Okay, Dad."

Meanwhile, down in Florida, my sis-in-law is self-soothing by putting up some Christmas lights — Corona Lites? In L.A., a mom I know is now listening to holiday carols.

"Silent night, holy night ..."

Sounds like my dating life.

Look, whatever gets you through the night. I try not to judge. Heck, I barely move. I've worn the same pair of PJs during my entire captivity. I sit around reading dog-eared Ken Kesey novels and listening to Kenny Rankin records. I thumb my ear as if there's a bug in there somewhere.

Doesn't really pay for me to be appealing to my captors. They are snarky and increasingly restless.

The other day, I revealed my complete confusion over Trader Joe's, how I'm probably the only person who doesn't worship rice cakes and all that weird dairy.

I was immediately swamped with suggestions for spatchcock chicken and goat cheese rolled in Argentine blueberries. Honestly, TJ's is just a parody of itself.

As am I.

I'm just glad there are things to joke about, and we still find reasons to smile.

Your honesty and resiliency impress me. My Twitter friend Gigi reports that she's growing out her beard.

"Me too!" my niece said.

I hear my buddy Bittner is building some sort of ark just in case. My attorney, Billable Bob, has taken up knitting. Big man. Sausage fingers. Good luck!

As I said, I don't judge. For two weeks, I have been drinking rum out of one of Posh's old riding boots.

And, sometimes, we're not coping so hot. Sometimes, we're all just a little scared.

My buddy Jay confesses to, just before sleep, doing a couple of test swallows and wondering: "Is that a sore throat?"

My daughter Rapunzel confesses to, once or twice a day, pausing to take a few deep breaths to test her lungs.

When I feel scared, I imagine striking out the '27 Yankees. I pitch Babe Ruth nothing but butterfly changeups and dirty curveballs. I zing him tight on the chin. He laughs a little and flicks the next pitch into the North Atlantic. Jerk.

Hey, let's promise not to fret more than we have to.

Eventually, the doors will swing open. In a month or two, we'll be dancing at weddings again.

And raising a toast to the most amazing thing of all: life.

I Miss church

D ear Diary,

I miss the bustle of churches on Sundays, the people scurrying down the sidewalks when they are late, and the families — some in clumps, happy in each other's company, others spread out and staring at their phones.

I wonder if that translates to home life now. Are some families clumping and others scattered with their toys?

Us, we're clumping, and I wouldn't recommend it. Our house is so cozy, we have little choice. We cook together; we play whiffle ball in the living room, something my late wife, Posh, would never have allowed.

The other day, my son put a baseball-sized hole in the garage wall while hitting balls into a net. I shrugged. A souvenir. A memory.

Another friend reports her son knocking baseball into neighbors' yards. I picture gardeners in coming months, leaning close, "What's this? A baseball?"

Better than any bloom. A baseball.

At night, we watch "Tiger King," a weird show for our weird times. Guess it's always comforting to discover other folks are weirder than we are, and we're plenty weird, just ask the neighbors.

Best case: They think we might be a cult.

I miss sports, but not as much as I thought. No junkie withdrawal. Only minimal tantrums and night sweats. This is a breather from sports, and I'm not sure that's all bad. We needed a national timeout from the fraggy 24/7 whirlwind of hype that modern sports have become.

The only thing that breaks my heart is the quiet of the Little League fields. No post-game pizza boxes half-folded in the trash, a very rich spring ritual. There are only so many years of that. Moms and dads need it as much as the kids.

Then there are the high schools, abbreviated senior years, missed milestones. Grief.

Other than that, do I miss sports?

Yes. I miss everything.

What I really miss are my daughters. Spotted one the other day, as you would a rare finch, just randomly, as we were moving my niece between apartments in Santa Monica.

Normally, moving is the worst thing in the world, but in our current idle state, it gave my son and I something to do. My niece didn't have many large items, and it was over too fast. When we were done, I wanted to move her again, maybe back to our house on the other side of town, where we had a pretty good "pod" going, as she recovered from her recent ACL surgery.

But my point was I saw my daughter during the move and couldn't hug her. I'm not much of a hugger to begin with; in fact, I pride myself on having pretty much shut down all emotions (they get in the way of my drinking).

But when you haven't seen your daughter in a while, it's natural to hug. Plus, she has a birthday coming up, and she's reaching that age — twenty-nine — where that's a tender, emotionally charged day. "Twenty-nine! Daddy, I can't be twenty-nine. That's almost thirty! And thirty is so old!"

You know the drill.

So I couldn't hug her and that bummed me out a little. Evidently, I'm a failed stoic. I need emotions after all.

My other daughter, the Princess Bride, won't see me at all, won't even get within range, fearful that I am some modern version of

Typhoid Mary, spreading misery and disease, and further postponing the major wedding that's already been postponed once.

"Think of the grandchildren!!!" she scolded me the other day.

For the record, we have no grandchildren. Or maybe we do. Who knows, it's been so long since I've seen her.

I also miss my friends. In fact, I miss my buddies the way I thought I would miss sports, on an almost hourly basis. Sure, I also miss my favorite funky bars, my barista, and my barber. I miss spontaneous conversations with perfect strangers, something I excel at. I can blab for hours to anyone about nothing, which is why I became a journalist.

But, man, do I miss my friends.

We've been good about keeping in touch. We text, we send silly videos. Basically, we have turned into 8-year-old boys.

I vow now, as another long week of this begins, to call a friend a day. They are no longer clumping. At this point, their wives and girlfriends are ready to kick them to the street. Or murder them.

But, as with my niece, I would gladly take these funny idiots in.

I might even hug one.

cabin
Fever

've noticed the geese going north again, a sign of summer, of normalcy, of moving on. They travel in pairs, no social distancing, no coughing into their elbows. The geese look to be almost holding hands.

I've always thought geese were the best lovers, great examples for the rest of us. They dress well. They travel a lot. They have a wonderful sense of romance. They even appear monogamous, but you never really know, do you?

Look, I refuse to give into the gloom and doom of the current Coronacaust. To be honest, I'm not even certain that all the closures are wise. Necessary probably. Not wise. Too authoritarian. Probably not even legal. Too much what Stalin would do.

We just don't know about this Charmin Virus, so we follow the rules and don't squawk too much. Yet contradictions are everywhere. We can't go to our wide sunny beaches, but it's fine to bunch up at the grocery. The hiking trails are closed, but the public buses keep moving.

Guess I need a good happy hour and a hearty handshake, two things that are a month away, maybe more.

"We are alone in this together," as one reader said. And when those simple social joys come back, we'll appreciate them even more. As with victory over Europe, we'll be kissing in the streets. Or nudging elbows. Hot!!!

Should've seen me on the boulevard the other morning, such a putz. Big strides, a fistful of flowers. I must have looked like the Statue of Liberty. They were for my pal Nancy, who's had it far worse than most of us.

Two months ago, Nancy was literally run over by a car — front wheels and back — while out for her daily walk. Walking was one of the things she loved most in the world, and now she can't.

Years ago, I wrote about a wedding and "the bride with the lemonade hair." Nancy is the bride's mother. Back then, there was lots of lemonade in Nancy's life. Now there are mostly lemons. Still, she smiles.

So I took her a big bundle of purple flowers, not sure the name. Picked them up at the farmers market. Each week, the farmers in our little suburb load up their pickup trucks and take their dairy and their produce to a little lot across from the park.

So good to see their hard work pay off. And it cheers me that the farmers markets are still open, as nearly everything closes. Now, they've locked down the loop around the Rose Bowl. Officially, the outdoors is off limits. Like Nancy, we're in a jail we didn't deserve.

We'll come through this together.

Till then, we make the best of things. It's the oddest thing for the boy and me, knowing we're stuck together indefinitely. Neither of us will take off to a ballgame or goof around with buddies this weekend.

We're hoping my daughter Rapunzel will drop by on her birthday. Is that a risk we can take? Is that a sign that life can go on? I mourn all the missed birthdays and bar mitzvahs. Imagine if you couldn't have a funeral? For the love of God ...

To keep my son laughing and entertained, I ask him dumb boomer questions about technology.

Is TikTok a clock?

What's a USB port?

Sometimes, the question is so clueless that he falls to the floor laughing, and I end up kicking him a little till he stops. In the ribs near his tickle spot. Evidently, a 17-year-old boy is one big tickle spot. And all ribs.

Sure, it's not a swanky life, but for now it is ours. Two geese, going north.

Is It over Yet?

t first, this was like camping. I raided the earthquake kit for ramen. Congratulated myself for stacking it in ways that didn't crush the noodles.

The big earthquake bin contained matches, candles, batteries and other essentials. Some of the cans had expired. But we were in the freaky early phases of long grocery lines and general insanity, and I didn't throw the expired cans out. Just in case, I kept them.

Silver lining: When this ends, we will all have updated earthquake kits.

Is it over yet? A reader's dad gave me that line. Evidently, that's one of the first things her father says in the mornings, a wry greeting, a wink of the eye. Dads, huh?

No, it's not over. But isn't that the thing that's on everyone's minds? Doesn't that sum up the global ethos? Is it over yet? Can I run out to Starbucks? Rub shoulders with strangers in some funky overstuffed saloon? Drop in someplace for sushi?

Food has been a salvation through this. Another silver lining: We no longer rush dinner.

I used to get home at night after two hours on the freeways, mad at the world, ornery over yet another domestic obligation. I'd throw something to eat together, then shovel it down as if it were a race.

Now, when 6 p.m. comes, I calmly start pulling out pots and pans and relish the idea of putting a meal together. When it's over, sometimes we just sit and chat for 20 minutes.

When my niece Amy and her boyfriend are here, we eat at the dining table, just like in the good old days of Posh. No one is in a rush to get up. Posh would've liked that. Moms, huh?

Is it over yet? Nope. Till then, we worry. We hold out hope. We self-medicate: Food. Music. Whiskey. Books.

Yesterday, I raided one of those little communal boxes where people donate and borrow books. I took the oldest one just on principle. Like us, a survivor.

Warning: I am kind of a weirdo in the first degree. I don't like Trader Joe's, and I despise rap music, celebrity profiles and boneless chicken wings.

For as long as I live, I will enjoy watching jet planes take off. In general, I have the attention span of a wet puppy. I make a joke of almost anything. I laugh at funerals.

With that warning in mind, I wonder whether we'll look back at this somewhat fondly one day, how we had more time for simple things.

I will never have a chunk of time with my son like this ever again. We may kill each other, sure. But before that, we're having a pretty good hang. We throw tight spirals in the yard and watch the silliest TV you've ever seen. We do laundry like Laurel and Hardy.

In fact, we have lots of Laurel and Hardy in our lives. You should see us try to cook together. We're both pretty lousy in the kitchen, which is a relief to me. Good cooks can be such bores and scolds.

We bump shoulders. We tease. We burn the fries. We scald the cheese sauce. Holy spit, I think the oven's on fire!

Again?

Really, it should be illegal for two goofs like us to cook. Yet we do. Badly and joyously. Strangely content in the stylish little kitchen his late mother loved.

Hey, is it over yet?

Books And Porridge

In our last episode, we suggested that we need to add good books to our emergency kits, and a bottle of Cabernet, some medical masks, a good football and maybe a sex toy.

Sorry, just making sure you are paying attention.

You awake now?

Look, I warned you I could joke about anything. To laugh at this awful pandemic, the same way we mock despots and tyrants, is to make it a little less powerful, to rob it of its muscle and ability to push us around too much.

Laughter is like porridge. Laughter is the best revenge.

My buddy Tom just told me a pretty good COVID-19 joke. I'd pass it along, but it takes two weeks to get.

I also just heard that in Panama they've resorted to separating the genders, allowing women and men to run errands on alternating days. I think that's wise, though I could just picture my daughters coming home with 20 purses and nothing to eat.

"Where's the milk, sweetie?" I'd ask.

"Milk?"

Me, I'd come home with 70 pounds of stew meat and a wheelbarrow of cigars.

Listen, if you really need a laugh, you should watch me on TV some night, on Spectrum, the cable channel that features a lot of really great *L.A. Times* journalists. And also me.

Helming the show is Lisa McRee, a television veteran, or so they say. Might be 55. Might be 30 — who can tell on TV? In any case, she's an amazing ringleader and still shows a childlike interest in virtually everything.

The other day, I was talking about dogs. Other *Times* guests talk about wars, epidemics and stimulus packages. I talk about how to adopt a good terrier mix in difficult times. Obviously, they understand my limitations. Honestly, I think they get some sort of subsidy to have me on.

Also involved — in the role of my TV spouse — is this really bossy, no-nonsense producer, Jennifer O'Hagan. Total pro. Probably falls to sleep each night wondering: "What's happened to my career? I'm really working with Erskine?"

Look, O'Hagan, as I told you, my dad was in TV. He was kind of a big deal actually, a producer and director of some note for CBS Sports. A colleague of his (Tony Verna) invented instant replay. The bunch of them invented the visual vistas of modern televised sports.

Exactly none of that rubbed off on me. I was, quite frankly, born 75 years too late, for I am a newspaper guy through and through. Mike Royko. Jim Murray. Breslin. Bombeck.

My words come to you still damp on the page. Like pasta. But straight from the heart. Each time I step away from the keyboard, I'm haunted a little by the fact that they should've been so much better.

That's print journalism. All journalism, really. Fast food.

They say papers are dying, but they've been saying that my entire career. I certainly hope not. A newspaper is my acoustic guitar. I love the rustle-rasp of the front page, like autumn leaves underfoot. I love the way newspapers struggle to tell the truth in a world that seems stacked against honesty and revelation.

In a world of spin, where there are 400 media reps for every one reporter, I love that there are still cranky journalists out there who traffic in the truth. I like that they are not polished, or blow-dried, or really suitable for television in the typical ways.

They are not "content producers." They are reporters. They actually leave the office. Most are better suited to cop bars and swanky hotel saloons, where the best tips come from anyway.

Most of all, I love that they are real. And that I've been able to work alongside them for more than 40 years.

And I love those of you who still support us, for better and for worse.

Breakfast Martinis

All is not lost.

Just heard that Brooks Brothers is knocking 30% off sweaters. Also noticed that the little kitchen shamrock we bought a month ago seems to be leaning toward the sun, as we all should.

And every morning, the leafblowers come, a very loud army, a belligerent band of two-cycled wasps descending on Los Angeles.

Every time you make a phone call, a leafblower starts up. Sometimes, they'll walk right into your house. Va-ROOOOOOOOOOM!

When it becomes particularly unbearable, I make a breakfast martini. Friends always quiz me: Gin or vodka?

I say: "Why not both?"

Look, it's up to each of us to fight the melancholy, the clamor, the ennui. I'm not even sure what ennui is. An oyster dish? Some sort of French soup? But I know we can't let it win.

These are the times we live in. The "make-the-best-of-things times," which is sort of what we always do, make the best of things. But we are challenged now like seldom before.

As the writer Paul Coelho said: "Life has many ways of testing a person's will, either by having nothing happen at all or by having everything happen all at once."

Why not both?

It is, after all, the weekend, though it kind of looks like any other day, doesn't it?

I've decided that I will manufacture some minor event — a rack of ribs, a water balloon fight — to mark the weekend.

I thought about putting up the Christmas tree, as one friend did, but decorating it with canned hams, in honor of Easter.

It's going to be a weird, wonderful Easter — I insist. The Easter Bunny is under quarantine, and I'm not sure we're allowed to line up at the Honey Baked store. What about eggs? Will there even be eggs?

At this point, I'm not even sure the farmers market will be open again. L.A.'s mayor seems to show a certain glee in locking things down.

Hey, maybe I'll bang out some bread.

Our friends the Hansens dropped off some bread the other day, a big powdered pillow of sourdough, with a jar of honey. I ate. I napped. I felt like Winnie the Pooh.

Never made bread before, but I've eaten tons of it. I understand that bread requires yeast, hops and water. No, wait, that's beer. Even better. I'll make beer in the bathtub. No one seems to be using it anyway.

Isn't it strange, the lack of showers? Without work to run off to or social events, America has almost completely quit showering. That's why it's important that I make bread. To freshen the air. I'll open the window so you can smell it. I'll set up a fan.

If a kid happens to come flying out of the window, that's just my son. I love him and all, but I toss him out of the house about three times a day. The other day, I expelled him from home school.

Yet hope and inspiration are everywhere, not just with Brooks Brothers sales, or shamrocks, or fresh-baked bread. The painted lady butterflies are starting to flutter about, clinging to the thistles like they always do.

Some residents have put up inspirational signs, and sidewalk chalk art — the color of butterflies — is showing up everywhere.

"Stay strong," it says. "We love you."

You don't even know me. But okay.

To stay busy, folks will do anything. The other day, we passed a husband and wife playing pickleball in their driveway.

Ever seen this new sport pickleball? Like tennis but smaller. I'm not sure where the pickles come in. But I like pickles, so I keep watching.

Just by coincidence, "Pickleball" was my nickname in college. I was telling my son all about this, and he asked: "What else did they call you, Dad?"

Some very nice things, obviously. Pee-Wee. Opie. Mork.

Oh, and this just in:

"So many people are getting sick of their parents," my son announced the other evening.

Really? It took this long?

According to my son, all the kids are kind of disgusted, but the college kids have been hit the hardest by this quarantine.

Yikes. I fall asleep each night worrying: "What about the college kids? Where will they go to smoke weed?"

Stay strong, kids. We love you. Remember, hope is everywhere. The butterflies are back. Good things await just ahead.

Because your old pal Pickleball is on the move, off to make a giant batch of sourdough bread. Or, better yet, beer.

Then I might decorate the Easter tree, with lights and glorious canned hams.

And do what we always do: Make the best of things.

Coffee Is My Courage

Dreary day. I mean they're all a little dreary lately. In this case, the sun's not supposed to return till Friday, which seems like forever. Like you, I enjoy the sound of rain on the roof. Just not all the time.

Lots of rain lately. April, as one friend put it, "might be the longest year of my life."

Coffee is my courage. The little nook where we keep the supplies looks prepped for combat. I drink a lot of coffee normally, but I drink even more now. After blood, it is my dominant fluid, my anti-freeze. Each morning, it puts bumblebees in my veins. It preps me every day for this stupid war.

I've also taken advantage of this lockdown to sample some of the Japanese whiskies. That has proven to be time well spent. Japanese whisky is smooth, like friendship ... like Miles Davis at midnight. When the bumblebees get the best of me, I turn to Japanese whisky.

Tough times. Fed-up moms have taken to pegging their insolent teenagers with potatoes, and in one popular video, a pot.

Clang. "Ouch Mom!"

"Can you hear me now?"

"No? Really?"

Clang. "Ouch!"

Me, I have no issues with my teen, as long as he does the dishes every other night and Swiffers the wood floors once in a while. This week will be interesting. It's spring break. I mean, did he really need a break?

"Yeah, Dad, I do," he said, in that teen twang that suggests you are the dumbest person in the world.

So I threw the couch at him.

Mostly, the kid and I get along. We stay close to home, in our cozy little house, with the American flag out front. Nice place. Used to be a Long John Silvers, so it smells a little like fried cod. But I've always liked fish.

I have to say, I love all the American flags I'm seeing, but I confess that I love the spring flowers a little more — the calla lilies, the roses.

I know the names of two, maybe three flowers, like I know the names of three composers, three presidents, a country or two. I hate those show-offs who remember everything. Relax a little. Enjoy.

So what I'm saying is the calla lilies are my Easter flags. A visual psalm, a rallying point on this unholy holy week.

I suppose every catastrophe has its iconography. At 9/11, it was the faces of the first responders. In this case, the dominant icon is facemasks. And if you're lucky enough, you can throw in a few Easter flowers.

In many ways, I think this catastrophe has brought out the best in us. It is the birth of a nation. Or a rebirth. On Holy Week, of all times. You could make soup of all the ironies. Throw in a few lilies. Some oregano. Bam! Soup!

Everything has changed. Eating has replaced yoga. Sweatpants and PJs are the new jeans. I realized the other day that I may never need to shop for clothes again. Think of the money I'll save. A hundred dollars a year, perhaps more.

Meanwhile, we have two friends with the crud now, and it seems to be creeping ever closer. One of the victims, a beloved former teacher, is in serious condition. Even if you don't pray, please mutter a prayer for her. It's a good time for hope and Hail Marys.

When isn't it?

I tell friends: Be well. Hang tough. Do the little things that give you pleasure. And reach out anytime ... "Really, anytime."

Of course, I don't really mean anytime. I sleep from 10 p.m. to 3 a.m., wake to pee, toss and turn awhile, fall back into a restless and sweaty sleep, wake up at 5 when our pet wolf tongue-kisses me on my snout, then rise happy and refreshed to dash off these little notes to you.

So what I mean: Reach out anytime — except between 10 and 5.

Also, try to let the trees and the tall grass embrace you.

On Sunday, I took White Fang on a long walk into the woods. Long grass. Four hundred shades of green. A concrete culvert nearby carried the first traces of a fresh storm ... my Irish Sea. It was sublime.

All sorts of wild flowers. I think even edelweiss, with their wooly white puffs, though probably only if we had hiked all the way to Switzerland. I seriously don't think we have edelweiss here, but I've seen a lot of unbelievable things lately.

Maybe it was edelweiss, a word you can hardly say without singing it.

Then we came upon a tunnel of trees. More than downtowns, more than Japanese whiskies, I like tunnels of trees, where the live oaks fold into each other, like the ceilings of cathedrals.

Yesterday, the dog and I lingered there a while. And said a prayer for our friend Terese.

Those Miserable Masks

My thoughts, as Woodsworth used to say, are "fed by the sun." But there isn't much sun this week, literally and in any other way.

It's amazing we even get out of bed, so bad the news. This week, more than most, they want us to stay home.

Who will buy the Easter ham?

I guess, like comics, like movies, Easter hams aren't so important in the entire scheme of things. We talked yesterday about icons, and holiday feasts are merely icons of the mouth.

Now that I think about it a little, Easter hams are really important. I think I'll brave the storms, put on my hazmat suit, and go get one.

Speaking of hazmat suits, I can barely even breathe in one of those simple little medical masks. My glasses steam up, and I get dizzy and wobble. Suffocation seems at hand — my worst fear.

I feel obligated to wear the mask, mostly for other people. Such a dad, right? There is no more selfless creature on the planet, other than a mom.

Honestly, I wish I had my mom and dad right now — for their toughness and their wise words. On the other hand, I'm glad they don't have to suffer this.

Look, life moves fast, and this country moves fastest of all. In no time, we'll be ordering root beer popsicles on toasty summer afternoons. We'll shove a canoe out on a spring-fed lake, drop a fishing line off a bridge.

I suspect that we'll also buy a lot of beers for total strangers who say the right things — who share a wry joke or find the fun in any situation.

That's what dads have always done and will soon do again.

Speaking of buying beer. I owe you one myself.

You have all been correspondents in these silly daily diaries. Little phrases and threads of things you share show up here, sometimes credited, sometimes not.

Yesterday, I said, "Coffee is my courage." But really, all of you are.

From one correspondent, Jill, in response to my love for tunnels of trees.

"You mention one of my favorite things I learned in landscaping school.

"In landscaping, an avenue, or allée, is traditionally a straight path or road with a line of trees or large shrubs running along each side, which is used, as its Latin source venire indicates, to emphasize the 'coming to,' or arrival at a landscape or architectural feature."

So when this is over, I owe you all a sweaty beer at my favorite funky saloon, the one with the red leather booths, a pool table, a juke box. And my old pals Bittner, Miller, Jeff and Big-Wave Dave.

All of us, all of you. My tunnel of trees.

Divine Light

As you know, I am a martini-is-half-full kind of guy, and I sense we are starting to turn the corner on all this. There has been an alarmist approach to the entire pandemic — and thank gawd for that. Because what did we know at the time, other than it could be a very gruesome thing?

But yesterday, I read that Gov. Bradley Cooper has given away 500 respirators to New York and other places, because the ICUs here are so slow.

First thought: "Whoa, pal, not so fast." But yeah, I'll take that as a sign and a generous gesture. From the orderlies to the governor, California has kind of nailed this.

So as Easter approaches, we have a bit of divine light. In many ways, it will be our most memorable holiday ever, even if we can't gather in the usual ways.

"Boys, we are going to come back on fire," texted my buddy Verge, who had the crud and is now on his feet again.

"That's not a pillow!" Wheels texted in response.

If you get that John Candy reference, you probably get us. It's not rocket science. Funny friends are more important than that. When things are at their worst, send in the clowns.

Verge reports that he mostly had a fever and a cough, never the awful breathing issues, though he confessed to moments in the middle of the night where he wondered: "How bad will this thing get?"

Listen, the middle of the night has been hard on all of us. It's just you and God in a dark room. You're a little pissy and a little scared. Both of you.

Then the dawn comes, and light and hope win out again.

Listen, I'm old — not ancient — but old enough. I graduated high school with Moses. For a short time, I even dated Helen of Troy. Nice girl. Didn't handle tequila well (which was all we really had in common).

Point is: After a long life of ups and down, all that I can promise you is this: In the end, the light always comes.

Lately, I have taken to leaving the comics pages strewn throughout the house so that my fellow pod mates — my son, my niece and her boyfriend — run across them randomly and have a quiet moment and a smile.

You know, just one of those stupid little things dads do.

After all these years, there is still something warm and cheesy-wonderful about a comics page — the scratchy drawings. They are like so-called "dad jokes" come to life.

I confess, I don't even get some of them (that's right, even the comics go over my head). And I can't even make out the tight eyelash font of "Doonesbury" anymore. I have to wait till Sunday when it's a little bigger. Then I shrug and say, "Meh, I don't know why I read "Doonesbury" anymore."

The answer: Because I always have.

When it comes to newspapers, we are scraping the bottom of the sugar bowl. One of the things I'll miss most: the comics.

What's refreshing about them right now is that they have yet to catch up to the pandemic. When they do, we won't have that little escape anymore.

Same with movies. What's especially good about them right now is there is no mention of masks or sore throats or respirators.

Like comics, they take you away. Movies lately are like holy water. Cleansing. Spiritual.

Drink of the week: Scotch and holy water. Cheers.

Remember Silly Putty?

The wolf was a little restless, so we took her for a ride.

Check out that face. The clown smile. The sheer joy. You can tell she's an Erskine, can't you? Did one of those doggy DNA tests on her once, and it came back "pure you. She's 100% you. And kind of an idiot."

A little idiocy is okay. Speaking of which, check out the final episode of "Modern Family" tonight. We don't have ballgames to look forward to, we don't have concerts. But, like the wolf, we need our anticipation and our laughs. "Modern Family" has provided a ton of laughs over the years.

In these wistful and uncertain times, we need to chase a few laughs more than ever.

"Watching the federal government deal with COVID-19 is like watching the Ministry of Magic deal with Voldemort's return," my buddy Roswell messaged.

Like Roswell, you gotta find the smiles. As we did with yesterday's post on the comics pages. That sure struck a chord. Everyone has a favorite. What a comfort zone.

To me, a comic is like a little motivational Post-it Note. If I set my coffee on the comics page, it stays warm.

My buddy Drucker recalls how, as kids, we used to peel off comic images with Silly Putty.

"The first memes," he said.

Another reader pointed out how much I resemble the beleaguered husband Dagwood in the "Blondie" strips. Matter of fact, my late wife thought so too. I remember how, in the most tender and personal moments, she would whisper, "Oh, Dagwood ..."

Wish she'd said it more.

One reader Wendy said she never took to *The New York Times* because it doesn't have a comics page.

And they call themselves a newspaper!

A random thought: Wonder if all the characters from the comics page came to life for a giant cocktail party with the readers who loved them? Or would that be too much like your typical family Christmas? Or our autumn tailgates?

Anyway, just a thought. Me, I'd head right for Calvin and Hobbes, then buy Charlie Brown his first beer.

Also, I think that you can get a good read on a job applicant — or a first date — by asking what comics they like. If they say they don't read the comics, politely excuse yourself and never come back.

My pal Andy points out how well the "Peanuts" comics hold up after all these years.

I'll go out on a limb here and say Charles Schulz was probably the greatest therapist America has ever had, surpassing Mr. Rogers and my bartender Chuey, who has also done some really outstanding work over the years.

Sometimes, all we seek after a long, baffling day is a nice nod and a cold martini. Or this week, Scotch and holy water.

Other therapists I'd like to thank: George Carlin, Richard Pryor, Steve Martin, John Candy, Albert Brooks.

Send in the clowns, baby.

Feasts of Flowers

Today's quiz: How do you know if you're going crazy when you're half crazy to begin with?

- Are you planning to use marshmallow Peeps in your potato dish?
- Are you talking to the dog even more than usual? (And does she answer you?)
- When the doomsdayers predict no football season this fall, do you feel just a little murderous?
- Have you recently made a Gucci face mask to match your bag?

If you answered "yes" to three of those, see a doctor right away. Oh, that's right, we're not supposed to leave the house.

Okay, call a doctor or text him in Latin. That'll get his or her attention. Latin, the dead language. Or the language of the dead?

The rain ends today, they say. Then the sun comes out, and I suspect spring will just explode.

On Good Friday, just wait till you see what God does with the cherry trees.

So quit waiting for your grumpy kids to wake up. They're mostly in hibernation, from what I can tell. Or on their phones.

My son married his phone yesterday. We had a small ceremony. I made a nice, teary toast. So far, they are very happy. But it's early. Too soon to really tell.

Point is, while they sleep, get out and walk a little. Check out those cherry trees. Get out and breathe.

Last night, three straight TV commercials ordered me to stay home: Jack in the Box was one of the companies, and Tylenol another. By the third, I was so sick of corporate America telling me how to behave that I can't remember which company it was.

I can just imagine the Zoom meetings that led to this: "In the ads, we should remind people to wash their hands," one executive probably said. "Make it seem kinda patriotic," another chimed in. "Make it seem like everybody is in this together."

Yeah thanks, you dolts.

By the way, one of my son's pals actually made a Gucci face mask. A USC girl stuck at home: I suspect she will make a small fortune selling them to the Chardonnay Moms in our loaded little town, who have been uncomfortable with the institutional look of the masks.

Disposable Gucci gloves, long ones for evenings out, cannot be far behind.

Anyway, starting right here, right now, I declare this "The Year of the Family."

Oh yeah, a lot of us are a little screwed up. In fact, we're all screwed up to some degree. Humans are naturally flawed. St. Augustine first told us about "original sin," and I remember reading that in college philosophy class and thinking: "Why even try then? Think I'll just go have a beer."

Take my family. Please? I'll pay you. One is getting married, another is thinking about it, the third doesn't want anything to do with long-term love, unless it involves dogs or baseball or his new bride, his phone.

There's a pet wolf and all sorts of odd aunts and uncles, cousins and more cousins.

They all have high-beam Irish smiles, and if you're not careful, they'll steal your wallet, but in that charming Celtic way in which you won't even feel fleeced. In fact, you'll feel grateful they took your wallet, and maybe offer them your car.

Take my car. Please.

We were talking about "tunnels of trees" the other day, and one reader mentioned that the best tunnels are the ones parents make after soccer games for the kids to trot through.

Good game, good game, good game ...

I think those are the moments that will finally heal us. Not holidays. Not TV ads. Those are the moments that will make us sane again, out in the sunshine, out in the company of strangers. Or on the patio out back, everyone over.

Meanwhile, on the front porch are two giant baskets of hanging flowers my sister bought us when she was here last month. Remember my sis? One day, she just willy-nilly threw out all my dead plants. The nerve.

Then she went and bought some new ones, two overloaded baskets of incandescent blossoms. They look like her hair, all this way and that. They remind me of her beautiful Irish smile.

So instead of family feasts this Easter, we'll have feasts of flowers. And we'll think brightly of the coming days when we can all hug again or just hang around doing nothing. Such a summer we're going to have.

Good game, good game, good game.

Hostage
Day 2,342

Sent the following note to a pal who had mailed me a heartfelt card reinforcing our brotherly friendship in these troubled times:

"Thank you for the card," I told him. "Very thoughtful. I hope that doesn't get to be a habit and we can soon get back to being our irreverent and silly selves. Love ya, man."

Will we ever be as silly and irreverent as we once were?

I insist. In fact, I'll devote my life to it. (Why change now?)

I sense that people are starting to become a little frayed around the edges. Me, I'm always a little frayed. With other people, it's more noticeable.

Shoppers are being bossy in stores, scolding total strangers over distancing. At Easter, a few of us gathered 10 paces apart, sat in chairs, had coffee, discussed rudeness, TikTok videos and other important things.

The lovely and patient daughter had a revelation, telling how she'd made "froth-ees," a combo of instant coffee, milk and sugar whipped together, in a cool and frothy breakfast drink. Froth-ees.

Finn, her fiancé, talked about how he'd made meatballs the night before by soaking breadcrumbs in cream, mashing them like snowballs with meat, and dunking them in a red sauce for 45 minutes.

With the Irish, the talk is usually either food or drink or books. We know almost nothing else.

Bad encounters at stores were also one of the topics, and my niece explained how some old guy was rude to her at the supermarket.

Dear old guy, from one old guy to another, back off. If I catch you being rude to anyone, let alone my daughters or niece, I will place you upside down in your shopping cart and shove you down a hill. Love ya, man.

Yeah, so even I'm a little frayed, I guess.

Good Easter though. My son and I filled Easter baskets for the daughters and the niece, loaded them with Peeps, flowers and Ghirardelli chocolates.

"What else?" I asked, as we assembled the baskets.

"Ammo?" he said.

Hmmmm, good suggestion, but in the spirit of Easter, we included a bottle of Yes Way Rosé instead, which seemed like something millennials would like. And they did.

Hey, you have to keep your fluids up.

The millennials have been drinking pretty steadily through this whole crisis, stuck at home as they are, missing the usual social outlets, like Egg Slut and Howlin' Ray's (a chicken place where, basically, they spray fire directly into your mouth).

So they're missing that. They are stuck with their live-in boyfriends. My daughter Rapunzel says she and her boyfriend are getting together fine, and the lovely and patient older daughter remains lovely and patient, despite being shut in with that funny meatball, Finn.

In fact, I think this lockdown has been good for couples. As long as you don't have kids around, this lockdown has been a pretty good test drive for a relationship. It answers, in a short period of time, some questions that otherwise would take years for couples to answer:

- Are you reliable in a crisis?
- Do you take your anxiety out on other people?
- Are you any fun?

I think if couples come through this, they can come through almost anything.

And if you have kids around? Well, that's another relationship entirely. Then the questions become:

- We made these little cretins?
- Would it be illegal to staple them to the wall?

Honestly, I love my little cretin. This will be good for us too.

Chardonnay Moms

n my defense, there was no weight listed on the Easter ham that I baked into oblivion on Sunday. There were directions: 10 minutes per pound. I looked and looked, couldn't find its weight on the elaborate packaging.

Guessed 20 pounds. It's just the two guys in the house, so we don't have a scale, though later, I remembered the luggage scale somewhere in the garage. By then, the ham was a goner.

It died twice, this ham. Once at some slaughterhouse Iowa, the second time in my oven.

Our Father, which art in Heaven, hallowed be thy name …

It's dry, sure, but there are options, as readers graciously pointed out. You can revive it with orange juice, cranberry juice or bourbon, though that seems a careless waste of good Kentucky hooch.

Look, a few of the interior slices are edible, and it'll be fine as leftovers, no matter what you do. I like leftovers best anyway.

Yesterday, in fact, I made a Peeps sandwich — blue Peeps on white bread. Really the most Caucasian experience possible, and I mean that respectfully. Some of my best friends happen to be Caucasian, and I treat them just like everybody else.

Someone suggested smearing the Peeps with peanut butter and grilling it, but I don't really like the symbolism of that. It would indicate some sort of Elvis-related eating disorder. He used to love fried banana sandwiches.

As Chelsea Handler said the other day: "I took a sleeping pill to stop from eating."

Another thing that made me laugh: the card our friends Jack and Paulette sent, of Jesus on Twitter: "12 followers so far. Sweet!" (mooningduck.com)

My post-Easter goal? To spend as much time working out as I do at the sink eating random stuff I find in my son's Easter basket. So far, the Easter basket is winning.

The problem is that it's the little things that sustain us right now. One Facebook friend said she's been putting marshmallows in her coffee. If that doesn't work, try a leftover Peep. The yellow ones pop out the most, and there it floats at the top of the cup, the way a duck would, before melting into the hot coffee.

Not that I've tried it or anything. But it's really yummy.

The other problem is that as I work out, running down the boulevard of our little town, passersby heckle me. Yesterday, it was Gary, the former pastor of our church, leaning out the window and chiding me to go faster.

Freaked me out. I suddenly felt pathetic, in the eyes of God and his top lieutenants.

I have the body of a young girl to begin with — no muscle mass, no heft — and though I run a lot, I've lost the manly rip in my shoulders that swimming used to deliver.

I love swimming. It's the most thorough cleansing you can have, and it does things for the arms and shoulders that you can't replicate with other workouts, such as lifting food to your face or reading *Esquire* magazine on the couch.

They closed the pool, so now all I can do is run. I run alone or with that idiot wolf. Passing drivers honk, or hurl insults or half-eaten food, like the apple they've been eating, or in one case, a half can of beer.

The Chardonnay Moms actually try to run me over when I jog, usually over some drunken quip I may have made, at a cocktail party years ago, about their kid's baseball swing. Over the decades, I've made a lot of drunken quips, and they've finally caught up with me.

Let's just say that there are a lot of Chardonnay Moms who hold grudges. At some point, we all have to move on. I'm running for my life out there. The last thing I need is some Range Rover rolling over my ankles.

In short, I am now the human version of my overcooked ham.

See how life ties together? One saga becomes another saga. So I will run, no matter what the local clergy says.

Besides, I like nodding to the pretty jogger with the slight overbite, Easter in her cellophane eyes.

I like seeing the rising sun slip over the mountains and the way the clouds clamp onto the damp canyons, in ways it never does at other times of the year.

How green are those trails right now, the ones that are roped off?

In my head, I write angry letters: "Dear Governor Hair Product. Trails and pools are essential services too. Please lift that trail ban as soon as you safely can."

I need my trails, I need my public pool. I can't outrun these Chardonnay Moms much longer. They're very determined people. Like Tiger Moms, but angrier, because their roots are showing, and their kids are driving them batty, and their husbands don't come out of the loo for days and days.

So they've got more issues than just me. I just happen to be a handy target. The whole thing kind of scares me.

As my buddy and former classmate Helgren texted me the other day:

"As is said in the Dune Trilogy: 'Fear is the mind-killer. Fear is the little-death that brings total obliteration.'"

I fear nothing except Chardonnay Moms. But I fear them a whole lot.

Risk Is Everything

Like you, we take a lot of walks. I've got ticks, I've got aphids, my knees are about to buckle.

The wolf, she takes her time on these walks. That's fine, for what else do I have to do at the break of dawn but stand in the cold rain on some country lane, staring at a tunnel of trees, hoping there's a light at the end.

I stand there and admire all the places that are better than mine: bigger, lovelier, draped in honeysuckle and taffeta ... with flecks of 14-karat gold around the doors. Four fireplaces, sometimes five.

I count the chimneys and think: "Five fireplaces, dude? Congrats. Can you lend me one?"

Our little house? All it's draped in is memories. There are whiffle balls in the gutters and a small garden and termites in the porch. I like it well enough.

And I am happy for the people with better houses. Sure, some married money, a classic life skill I learned too late.

But I'd like to think most earned their fortunes in some admirable way — crushed it at the office, took more risks, which is something they never teach you in school. To take risks.

Risk is everything. Without it, there are no jackpots, no big rewards. Nothing gets better.

That's my theory on risks, use it as you will. After all, I am just a man standing in the dark with the dog, the cold rain tingling down my neck.

Me, I took plenty of risks. None of them panned out, except for having too many children. That might be the riskiest thing of all. And the biggest jackpot.

This weekend, if not for the current crisis, would've been my older daughter's wedding.

That doesn't mean we're sad. Life is tears and laughter. She will be married another day, most likely in June, though we're not certain yet the year.

But when the crisis lifts, what a wedding we will have. There will be a keg, a live band, lots of square dancing.

"You know what people like?" I told my daughter the other day.

"What, Dad?

"Root beer Popsicles," I said. "People really love root beer Popsicles."

And I'll make a teary and hilarious toast.

If there's anything an old mick like me can do, it's give a wedding toast to the most wonderful daughter a dad could ever have, scary smart and radiant as candles on Christmas Eve.

Posh would've liked to be there, of course, and we may leave an empty place setting and a red rose to honor her, maybe fill her wine glass a little.

It will be wistful, it will be wonderful. She will be remembered every time her oldest daughter smiles.

A mother's daughters are the heartbeats she leaves behind. And her sons too, though the daughters tend to be a little less feral, a little more like them.

I'm not going to bash boys here, because I'm really sick of that. Besides, if you have a son, you have everything.

Take my son (please).

He's on his fourth week home from school, and one moment we are sidekicks, the next we are hurling chairs at each other from across the room.

Lately, he's been beating me at more and more games. It's the natural order of things. First, sons beat dads at driveway basketball, generally around the age of 15.

Then they start remembering sports stats better than you, their brains like bear traps.

Then one day, they are taller. That's the worst.

Eventually, they beat you at board games too, and that's what's happened lately, the little idiot showing less and less remorse with every victory.

Really starting to get to me. I've devoted my life to him, and if you asked him my age, he probably wouldn't come within 30 years. I'm not even sure he knows my first name.

Still, I love him, even though he keeps beating me at Jenga, the stackable wooden puzzle.

Usually, he wins by kicking me under the table or breathing hard when it's my turn.

His favorite trick is to mimic my heart rate while I tenderly try to extract a puzzle piece, as if it were a kidney.

"Ba-BUMP, Ba-BUMP," he says, trying to make me twitch.

It sounds like the soundtrack from "Jaws," the way he does it, steadily faster. Baaaa-BUMP ... Baa-BUMP ... Ba-BUMP ...

Like life, the gag gets funnier every time he does it. Yesterday, he beat me twice, the Jenga pieces tumbling to the table. The ruins of Rome. Or his bedroom.

So here's to all the things in life that we build up, knock down, and build back up again ... that's our nature and our need.

And here's to all the tingles — the things that make us happy, and by "things" I mean people, especially the two auburn-haired daughters in lockdown on the other side of town.

Yep, dear God, this would've been her wedding day.

Ba-Bump.

Eternal Flames

Never told anybody this — not even the kids — but the candles on the mantel represent the four children and my late wife.

Like summer, I thought I could always count on her, that she'd always be around, relentlessly because she was a relentless person. Then cancer came.

Now, each night at 5 p.m., her candle springs to life, an electronic anode firing electrons at a semiconductor. A diode stirs.

And, like that, she lives and breathes again.

Hardly as romantic as a real wick. But reliable, you know? I'll settle for reliable right now. After all, summer is coming, and I need her around in this small way.

The four other candles kick on too at that point — at 5 p.m., the hour when people usually begin arriving home. They represent my two daughters, my two sons.

One of them is gone too, except in this votive sense. All there really is left of my late son are his ashes, his crazy wolf-dog, a snowboard in the basement, and this battery-powered candle on the shelf.

From Target. You can get them cheap at Target.

If he were alive, my son would make a joke of trying to blow it out each night, and hyperventilating when the LED candle would keep burning. That kind of idiocy is what I miss most about him, probably. He was the funniest guy.

He'd laugh at how things are now, so bad they're funny.

I read about people being rude in stores, or short with strangers on the street, or stressed and crappy and generally awful, and I think how lucky I am that I don't live with people like that — people who are rude and awful on a random basis.

If anything, my family is nicer to strangers than they are to me. I think a lot of families operate that way. Their default is to be nicer than you have to be.

The difference? Were you raised, or did you just grow up? Did you have loving parents? Did they insist — no, demand — that you be kind and patient and decent with loved ones and other people?

Meanwhile, we are now all like restless racehorses waiting for the bell to ring and the starting gate to burst open. We've done all the chores, ironed the Thanksgiving linen, organized the DVDs alphabetically (and by genre), changed the oil in the mower.

We survived Easter in isolation only by knowing that May could be sensational, that all the rain and snow would nourish the lawns and gardens, and that we would appreciate them in stirring ways, like Woodsworth did, of those dancing daffodils by the lake.

I gazed — and gazed — but little thought
What wealth the show to me had brought ...

We will go out to get our hair cut — what a haircut that will be. I suddenly look like Ted Koppel, a mop on top that I tilt down as I speak to my son, who has even more hair. We are both prisoners of our own hair, like two dudes left too long in a dungeon.

Seriously, if my hair gets much longer, I'll have to fire up the mower.

Best of all, when this is finally over, we'll have people over to the house again.

On the mantel, the candles will flicker to life.

And we'll all be together laughing, in the soft light of other people.

Hard Honest Truths

We were talking yesterday about how you can remember people with candles, particularly the battery-powered kind that spring to life each evening, as you read or drink or cook.

I do all three simultaneously, by the way. As a single parent now, I am always multitasking. Otherwise, we wouldn't eat, or the laundry wouldn't get done, or dust bunnies would overrun the house. Once they start breeding ...

Never does an hour go by where I'm not attending to some little thing.

So yeah, I got a little sappy yesterday, with the candles and all. The fireplace is the focal point of our cozy little house. It's where the logs glow and my heart beats. That's why I keep the candles there, as daily tributes to my wife and kids.

"You should put one up there for yourself," someone suggested. But I already think too much of myself, a writer's curse, or anyone's curse. In truth, I'm lucky to have all those domestic chores to attend to.

"I buried my husband's ashes under a rose bush in the backyard," my Facebook friend Jean said. "Every time it blooms, I'm sure he is with me."

That'll top a candle any day.

Little Globs of Sad

Each day, words go back and forth. I write something, then you write something back. It's like we are tag-teaming life right now. Helps to be able to call on the wisdom of the choir.

You know, writers are spies. We hope to notice stuff about life that we think no one else does, then make a big deal about noticing it, only to discover everyone else in the world has already spotted it.

That's writing ... giving voice to our little secrets. Then finding out there are no secrets. I wouldn't recommend writing to everyone. It's a lousy thing to love.

On the candle thing, I blame Harry Chapin.

The boy and I have been making dinner together, usually accompanied by hits from the '60s and '70s — are you surprised? Like me burning the Easter ham, the only thing that would shock you is if I didn't still listen to music from the '60s and '70s, the American Renaissance.

The other night, some soulful troubadour came on — Harry Chapin, or maybe Stephen Bishop — and my 17-year-old son says: "Whatever happened to music like this?"

Gordon Lightfoot followed, with a voice like a giant tree, the notes starting somewhere in Middle Earth.

And my son said: "What a voice."

Not sure I ever loved him more than at that one moment.

So I get up the next day, read a little Wordsworth, and start writing about candles. Lord help me, I'm turning into Emily Dickinson.

Then the words start to go back and forth. Lori Corbin talks about moments in life that leave us with "little globs of sad" in the throat.

Thanks, Lori, for out-writing me. Nothing in the candles piece tops "little globs of sad."

Sylvia Ramos Valle wrote: "In Spanish there is a phrase 'toca el corazon.' Translation "touches the heart" — which doesn't come close to the true meaning. It's a knock the wind out of me/brought me to my knees meaning. You, sir, have touched my heart once again."

Sylvia, I think you just out-wrote me too.

But it's not a competition ... I was never too good at those anyway, unless it was a game of pool at midnight, after too many beers, with a jukebox in the corner playing Waylon ("Belle of the Ball" was always my favorite).

As with Waylon, there are a lot of hard, honest truths flying around right now.

This has been a poetic moment for America, awful and inspired, the kind of moment that taps some deeper recesses. The stuff we usually conjure up at midnight over too many beers.

"We've lost them and yet they are with us. It's counterintuitive — our lives are studded with opposites," Jean wrote of the loved ones we lose.

"Pain is universal, happiness not so much," Kathy noted.

Good point.

Of course, I want to remind you that gin and tonic season is upon us. My daughter's fiancé, Finn, the dancing Irishman, mentioned that the other day.

Apparently, back in high school, Finn had a teacher who proclaimed the Saturday of Easter weekend as the start of gin and tonic season.

That feels of sea spray and great music, teak tables and the sound of ice clunking into good heavy glasses.

It makes me think of paddles thudding against the side of a canoe. Of someone starting up the grill. Of sunsets that last three days.

Me, I'm going to go buy some limes right now. These days, it pays to be prepared.

Because they can take away baseball, and torment us with the possible loss of football, which would be like a pubic beheading.

They can talk about keeping us apart, of turning day-to-day life into a fretful series of precautionary measures. They can even mess with my daughter's wedding.

But Governor Hair Product can't take away our gin and tonic season.

Carpe noctem. Seize the night.

Feel the glow.

More Gin & Tonics

True confession: I write these just to read your comments, which seem to feed — or water — my imagination, lend a social element to a somewhat isolated life, let me into your heads a little, give me fodder for the next episode.

I love you, is what I'm saying. And it's kind of a physical thing.

Last night, I dreamed I was that sparkling gin and tonic I wrote about yesterday. Handsome drink, right? And it enjoys a lot of lips.

I was seeking a summer style anyway, so a gin and tonic will be my inspiration: shorts, polo shirt, light sweater, and a gin and tonic in a big flower vase.

That's how I roll in summer. I drink from flower vases. I let my hair go a little. If I knock on your door some evening, don't let me in. I'll never leave.

"There's a man I know who makes a gin and tonic that sneaks up on you," my buddy Murph wrote. "You're happily sipping this nice little drink, chatting with him and enjoying life, and the next thing you know, you can't feel your fingertips."

I am that man.

Note, as Lisa Klein did, that if you add a spear of cucumber to your G&T, you've met your daily quota of vegetables.

Another reader pointed out — I forget just who — that alcohol is a disinfectant. Use that info accordingly.

Feeling good today, thanks for asking. The weekend is here, finally. What a week it was. I burned the Easter ham, invented the Peeps sandwich ("Looks like you're killing Smurfs," my old high school pal Vicki said).

We chatted about the notorious Chardonnay Moms, who run our suburb, and mocked Governor Hair Gel, who thinks he runs the world.

And how about the mayor, suggesting we're on lockdown through football season?

Yeah, good luck with that, pal. Listen, you both did fine. Now it's time to loosen the reins.

Lately, I've been throwing the football in the park with the boy a lot. He and I are like a sequestered jury. It'll come as no surprise that I get on his nerves more than he gets on mine.

We've been breaking for lunch in the park, which is open — KEEP YOUR DISTANCE! KEEP YOUR DISTANCE!

The weather is glorious, and the grass is thick, like spring lambs. You're quickly up to your ankles in the curly green wool.

So we kick off our flip-flops and toss the football. I throw a pretty tight spiral, though sometimes I let the tip drop, and it turns into a fluttering pheasant.

By the way, my son is so skinny that I worry about him a little. When he's backlit, you can almost see right through him, the spleen, the ribs, all the various bladders, the penny he swallowed when he was 2.

Poor kid. He's stuck with my cooking, after all, and I wonder whether he'll ever fill out. Or will he forever look like the kid in the "Zits" cartoon?

Then he flings the football, in high and mighty arcs. The ball glances off the sun, then drops into my soft suburban hands.

Score.

He is the only person I can hug these days, and if I had to pick just one, he'd be it.

You know, there are things I like about these weird times, I won't lie. I'm not on freeways. There are fewer meetings. My bar tab is down to nearly nil.

I like that I have two hours to spend on burning our dinner each night.

People ask: "What's your secret in the kitchen?" I say that I wait till all the smoke alarms in the house go off.

"It's done!" I scream.

"It's on fire," my son says.

"Same thing," I say. "Let's eat!"

I also like spending quality time with the pet wolf.

"My, what big ears you have, Grandma," I tease her.

She just tilts her head and looks at me in the puzzled way of pets. My goal before this lockdown is over: to teach the wolf to laugh, though I fear I need better material.

Toughest audience ever: White Fang Erskine, a 4-year-old husky that might be a wolf, might be my French mother. Humorless, unless it's her own joke, then she laughs a little too loud.

"You have to understand, I was raised by Audrey Hepburn," I told the wolf last night after my second gin and tonic.

She laughed.

Have a weekend. Get some sun when you can.

Jesus
Holy God

Oh no. I thought they meant *fattening* the curve. The other day, I found that my jeans fit fine without a belt. Used to be, before the Coronacaust, that I needed a belt. Them were the days.

Now, I'm two months pregnant, and my grammar is fractured. I fear my brain may be rotting just a little. Twice, I've forgotten my wallet lately, and on Saturday, I referenced Lennon and McCartney during a phone conversation with a friend, but I called him McCarthy. As in the famous writing team of John Lennon and Joe McCarthy.

Jesus holy God.

I didn't stop to correct myself, just raced through the reference hoping my pal Curwen didn't notice. But he noticed. He's just too decent a guy to call it to my attention. Yet, later, over drinks, I know it will come up. I just focus on the good — that later, there will be drinks.

We're all a little wounded in this, with worry, with social isolation. I am rooming, it appears, with what appears to be an actual orangutan (my teenage son).

In fact, I followed the advice of another dad over the weekend and tried to staple-gun my son to the wall. But if you don't catch his sleeves just right, or the cuff of his pants, they'll wiggle loose, and then you have a pubescent ape jumping around the house again.

"Eat the ape!" I keep telling White Fang, our wolf. But she won't go near the kid, for good reason.

At breakfast, my son was telling me he found a good deal on some sweatpants — the new national uniform — and could he get some, since they were so dirt cheap and all.

"How much?"

"Sixty-three dollars," he said.

"Wow, that's a great price," I lied.

I guess $63 isn't a bad price for sweatpants, though that's about what I used to spend on suits, when I would buy suits, which I don't anymore. I don't buy anything these days, except food and gin.

In our last installment, I noted how gin and tonic season had begun, a small reason to rejoice, or at least a tactic for rejoicing, when we don't have much to rejoice about.

Over the weekend, I went to 7-Eleven and bought a lime — I get all my fresh produce there. Then, with gin adding a rare clarity to my thought process, I decided that I'm forming the "Gin & Tonic Society of Greater Los Angeles." We'll apply for non-profit status, lots of grants and maybe some fellowships.

Hope you'll consider one day joining the Gin & Tonic Society of Greater Los Angeles. We might get hats made!

In a weak moment, my former colleague Sam agreed to serve as Mistress of Social Outreach, an unpaid position but an important one.

She's a lanky sort, a Hitchcock blond, with a taste for gin and a professorial knowledge of local gin joints. I told her we needed a hangout for the club, someplace a little swanky but not too nice.

"Maybe a place that peaked in 1984, like me."

"I'm on it, chief," she said.

So we have that to look forward to.

Meanwhile, the monkey just dropped his phone in his yogurt, despite my telling him not to futz with his phone during breakfast and "put it down for once."

"Sorry, Dad," the monkey said.

Big deal, a little yogurt.

For the record, I expect his behavior to improve tremendously when he gets that new pair of $63 sweatpants.

So yeah, we had a rockin' weekend. Saturday would've been my daughter's wedding, so there was that sad little milestone to plow through.

We Zoom-toasted her and her fiancé, Finn, promised each other that it will end up better than ever, when/if the marriage ever happens, which it will, we know it will.

We've been through so much worse that a little wedding delay doesn't seem quite so awful as it otherwise might.

Then on Sunday, the boy and I filled the car with petunias and verbena and dropped them in my daughter's front yard for her. She's good in the garden and wanted to fill a few flower boxes in her Santa Monica bungalow.

So we dropped off some potting soil too, and some other plants with the cowboy name of Dusty Miller. I like that name: Dusty Miller.

"I knew a Dusty Miller once," I told the boy.

"Really?"

"He used to rob stagecoaches," I lied. "East of Bartow."

And that's how our weekend went. Jesus holy God.

Dark Times.
Dark
chocolate.

I found, as I just made my coffee and fed the wolf, a chunk of leftover cookie dough in the fridge, and I thought — as I often do — "why the &%$#@)&*&% not?"

I usually add a thimble of sugar to my coffee anyway, and lately I have a sweet tooth, dating back to Easter, when I filled the kids' baskets with dark chocolates and wine.

My daughters kept the wine and tossed the chocolates, leading to my sudden fixation with dark chocolate. Dark times, dark chocolate.

It gives me inexplicable little jolts. Like the first time I saw Grace Kelly.

So now, in addition to having just founded the Gin & Tonic Society of Greater Los Angeles, I have given the world cookie-dough coffee. This is a creative binge unlike anything I've ever experienced. If this keeps up, I might write a book or something. Or needlepoint a new car.

Or write a column worth keeping.

I was humbled yesterday by that video Amanda McBroom sent honoring America.

I get bored with a lot of things people pass around, but this was extraordinary. Dare you not to cry (in a good way).

This purgatory we're having seems to sort of dare you not to cry. And how do I respond? I offer cookie dough coffee and a video made by someone else.

Oy. At least it's something.

Have to say, I like this new trend of offering little unexpected gifts — I hope it becomes an American tradition, something the Swedes talk about when they visit: "So, these Americans, they just drop off gifts for no apparent reason?"

Lately we do. I've received random bottles of wine, cards and sourdough bread with a jar of honey.

In return, I've left bundles of farmers market flowers on porches. In Bittner's case, I gave him a rack of barbecued ribs.

You didn't expect normal gifts from me, did you?

I have to tell you that my buddies are itching to get out again, and just itching, for that matter. I'm not sure half of them even bathe, to tell the truth. They smell like those earthy hippie women I used to date in the '70s.

Point is, they've had enough of this quarantine.

"I say we throw the watches in the ocean and dream of what was," Big Wave Dave texted, which sounds a lot like what those hippie women used to tell me when they were stoned.

What's your breakout plan? What's the first thing you want to do when life loosens up again? Get a haircut? Catch a movie? Surf? Hike? Canoodle?

What will you do after you hurl your watch in the ocean?

Me, I'm going to smoke a rack of ducks and make a batch of gin and tonics. I'll invite a few buddies over, maybe a few of the wives.

Not their wives, necessarily. Just random wives. They're everywhere in our little town, and I have to assume they'd like some gin and smoked duck.

Look, if this quarantine goes on much longer, I'll start making pottery. I don't like pottery. I don't like making it, don't like looking at it.

Pottery reminds me of the hippie girls I dated, who were into hemp cigars and pottery and sex in the woods.

I told Big Wave Dave that if I start making pottery, to just put me in a rowboat and push me out to sea.

"Okay," he said, and went off looking for rowboats.

So now, I'm a little worried. Big Wave never picks up on nuance or any figure of speech.

Honestly, I miss my buddies: Bittner, Big Wave, Billable Bob, Jeff, Verge, Gino, Pete, Siskin, Chris, Tom, Jon, even Miller. Plus all the guys from my Sunday afternoon football game. Plus my hiking club. Plus Miller. Did I mention Miller? He goes crazy when I leave him out.

They are the best buddies a dope like me could ever have.

When I lost my son in a car accident, they rallied 'round us like you wouldn't believe. Bittner stopped by one day and planted a tree in the yard.

It now blooms better than any tree I know. Like my late son, it's big in the shoulders.

Like my buddies, it is there for me. As I will be for them again.

Very soon, guys. Very soon.

The Marriage Test

This whole mess seems Orwellian, right? How you can no longer hug the people you love? If you smile in public, no one can see it through your mask. Maybe your eyes twinkle a little, which could be mistaken for a low-grade fever.

Odd times we live.

It feels like World War III one moment and an extended Christmas break the next. For most of us, it is only a major inconvenience. For others, a threat to our very existence.

It's easy to laugh at all the toilet paper shortages and such till you realize folks are scared out of the wits. Or worse, dying alone in the chill sheets of some hospital without their loved ones at the bedside to caress their foreheads.

That goes beyond Orwell. That is some sort of Twilight Zone. For the first time in my life, I couldn't open the Sunday paper. The world was awful, and I'd seen enough.

The good news, three days later? All sorts of tiny kindnesses have emerged from this, as well as a medical valor unlike anything we've ever seen.

And when did you ever think the clerk at the checkout counter would be hailed as a superhero?

"Test them," my sister insists. "It's a giant petri dish. If you want to see how prevalent this is, they should just test the workers in the checkout lanes."

I like when my sister is right. When this is over, she should receive some sort of honorary medical degree. Or be named surgeon general.

I just sent my sister a photo of the hanging baskets she bought us when she was here in March, just as the crud was emerging. I told her the flowers were getting better every day.

That often isn't the case with hanging baskets of flowers. Generally, they are like us. They peak young, great bonnets of blossoms, then slowly lose their childlike luster. Their posture sags. But these flowers are getting stronger every day.

Just like us.

Each day is a little better, right? This epidemic could've been so much worse, and now we're getting better, in baby steps, in incremental ways that are barely discernable. But we are getting better.

Yesterday, I was putting a lot of crud in my coffee: cookie dough to start with. Then, as the day progressed, I added chocolate, bourbon, marshmallows, mollusks.

At one point, I think I roofied myself. I was drowsy and disoriented, sort of my normal state. I fell asleep in my own arms.

Then I rallied. There is now an empty jar of peanut butter on the nightstand near my bed. Cause for alarm? No, a cause for celebration. I've found that nothing satisfies the appetite quite so much as finishing a jar of processed peanut spread in one sitting.

Try it.

Cured the blues. And it gave me the strength to overeat at dinner.

Last night, I made tostadas and drank Dr Pepper, who, by the way, is not covered under my medical plan but should be. Dr Pepper is the best soft drink of all and should be in everyone's medical plan.

As should gin, though I have no defense of that, other than it makes me feel better. Governor Hair Product will probably outlaw gin very soon, given his natural inclination to suppress us in every way.

But the gin and the peanut butter worked out. By the end of the day, I was emailing random people and asking them to marry me.

I think that's a baby step. I'm feeling romantic again, while spreading the feeling of fresh love and hopefulness to others, whether they like it or not.

In the past — long, long ago — I dated seriously and well before marrying. I no longer have time for that. Now, it's short and random courtships I'm seeking. As good an approach as any.

Life is tough; marriage is tougher. I'd like to think this long lockup will actually improve many marriages, because it is yet another unpleasant situation you've shared. Like having kids.

Having kids bonds you, right? Like corona, it's a warlike experience. Who else will ever understand the things you went through raising kids, or care enough to fete them on their birthdays, or go crazy with pride when they finally graduate from college in six years instead of four?

No one, that's who. And this is another one of those shared life experiences. So you may as well hold onto the spouse you have. Hope that happens.

Yep, good little things are happening all around us, in those incremental ways that are barely discernable.

Go celebrate a little. The peanut butter is right over there.

Silverstein
And
Shakespeare

They are both beautiful animals ... the wolf ... the boy. "Of hand, of foot, of lip, of eye, of brow ..." as Shakespeare said. They have that outer glow of youth and an inner restlessness.

Me, I just have the restlessness. Glow fled me years ago.

Where did glow go? Sounds like a Shel Silverstein poem, right? Shakespeare and Silverstein. They shared a kind of mirth. Like vodka and vermouth. Like gin and tonic. Shakespeare and Silverstein. It should be some kind of cocktail they serve at the Biltmore.

The wolf rests next to me as I write this, a kind of muse, a type of foot warmer. I try to finish these stupid notes before the sun comes up. It gives a certain urgency to the writing, a false deadline to propel me along.

If you've ever worked for a newspaper or a TV station, you know all about false deadlines. If you need a story by 8 p.m., you tell the reporter 7 p.m. If he or she is young, 6 p.m.

That's how you get your story at 8 p.m. It's a small wisdom, an acknowledgement of need vs. human nature.

So, up I get, each day in the dark, with my false deadline and my coffee, a big old cup you could almost do laps in. When it is done,

I am done. Then off for a walk we go, the wolf and I. It's not a bad way to start a day.

I'm not sure how much longer I'll do these morning posts. They seem a tad repetitious at this point. I have other, more important things I should probably be doing at 5 a.m. — a book, the laundry.

The bathrooms need a sponge bath. The dishwasher needs some tender, loving care — there's something wrong with the drainage vent. I've been trying to figure it out for five years, and the longer it goes unsolved, the more determined I get.

There is no home project that, given a wrench and a few hours, I can't make even worse.

Still, we seem to be discovering new things about each other. There was that cookie-dough-in-the-coffee revelation the other morning, and now we have the Gin & Tonic Society of Greater Los Angeles, which has been a rallying point for a lot of people, even me.

I think it's the lime. But, who knows, maybe it's the gin? My old pal Sam — the Hitchcock blond — has agreed to be the club's Sorceress of Social Outreach, or some such. Whatever we do, we need to see that play out.

You folks seem unexpectedly excited by this new club, which I think is very revealing of your character, in a good way. You have suggested about 100 flavors of gin. Who knew there were so many gins? That could take me days of study. But, as with the dishwasher, the longer it goes, the more determined I get.

Then there was all that stuff about peanut butter, which was another call to arms.

As it turns out, lots of you have very strong opinions about peanut butter, some even insisting that I try the organic brands, which I find unacceptable. The organics cost twice as much and seem to sweat and separate in the jar.

Give me Skippy any old day. Or even a supermarket generic. It is real, like boot leather, like acoustic guitars. As with gin, there are little truths in every jar.

"Hey, try making peanut butter cookies," Kathleen wrote. "Before baking, sink your thumb in the center and fill with jam when just out of oven."

All I can say to that is: "Kathleen, will you marry me?"

Barb suggested a sandwich of peanut butter and thinly sliced sweet pickles.

I mean, how does that even happen? I understand how Sonny found Cher. Even how Lyle Lovett found Julia Roberts. But not sure I'll ever understand how peanut butter came to marry sweet pickles in a sandwich.

But, sure, I'll try it. Thanks, Barb!

"If you pull out the middle stamen on your flower buds, they have sweet nectar on the stamen," Mary wrote. "Could go well with your peanut butter!"

Listen, Mary, I'm not going to start going around yanking out random stamens. I've been on the other side of that far too often. Once you start with stuff like that, where does it stop?

Wonder if the nectar is addictive? With me, lots of nectars are addictive.

Bruce Fishman says: "Try cream cheese with sardines or jelly."

Leave it to a Fishman to suggest sardines.

This is what I do for significant chunks of the day — read your silly feedback. Yet there's hardly a single suggestion I don't try. It's almost become an alternative lifestyle. Need vs. human nature.

Look, I lead a simple life of simple pleasures. After I mentioned Dr Pepper, the greatest medical man of our time, my old pal Kimberly informed me that Dr Pepper makes an ice cream syrup.

That alone is reason to get up in the morning: the knowledge that 16 hours later, I would have a small bowl of vanilla ice cream topped with Dr Pepper syrup.

Lord, that might be better than gin. Next up: The Dr Pepper Club of Greater Los Angeles.

The ultimate takeaway from all the feedback is that you are all a little too smart for me.

"I've been reading Albert Camus's The Plague," Debbie said. "Amazing how relevant it is."

"You used the word 'crud' several times in your post," Debbie wrote. "Here's one word I learned from this book — 'recrudescence.' It means recurrence of an undesirable condition, especially in context of disease. Possible dark post for dark moments."

Thanks, Deb. I'm trying to avoid dark posts for now. I like to get up at that moment when dark turns to light, and go to bed when gin turns to tonic.

So far, that's working out for us ... the strapping boy and this very pensive wolf. Leave it to me to have a pensive pet wolf.

At night, she grows quiet as I grow quiet. When we have ice cream, she has ice cream.

And, together, we toast another day.

survival
Lists

Five reasons to live:

- Dr Pepper and creme soda
- Peanut butter right out of the jar
- Posh's chicken chili*
- Vintage car shows on summer evenings
- Fluffernutter sandwiches (peanut butter and marshmallow crème)

We have become, in these troubled times, connoisseurs of small and silly pleasures, little joys that I hope we can all turn to in future troubled times.

Not that there will be any. No way. In the last 20 years, we've pretty much used up our quota.

I worry for my son, who knows only this century, a century of troubled times. But what does he really know? This is his only frame of reference, and his head is filled with friends and baseball and all sorts of wonderful mental mementos of his late mother and brother.

Yet you have to hope there are better, calmer days ahead for him and us, that humanity and science will figure this out, that we'll all learn to start giving the benefit of the doubt to the other side, and not be so smug and sure of ourselves.

If there's one thing I know about someone who's too sure of himself, it's that he probably knows nothing at all.

What goes around, comes around. Seen it so many times. Just the other morning, I was walking the wolf and ignored a ketchup-stained wrapper someone dropped on the sidewalk.

Normally, I would stoop down, throw it away. During the Coronacaust, I didn't necessarily want to pick up someone else's lunch litter. But the wolf? She had no hesitation, and soon I was wrestling it out of her mouth and dropping it in the trash after all.

Karma seldom works so swiftly.

But it works. Often, there are long gaps between the infraction and the penalty. But there seems to be some sort of cosmic-justice force field that eventually sorts these things out. You just have to hang in there. Hanging in there is its own reward.

Five more small and silly pleasures:

- The Gin & Tonic Society of Greater Los Angeles
- Hash-brown potatoes
- The Happy Hour Hiking Club
- The feeling beach sand makes when it squishes between your toes
- The Sunday comics

The other day, I warned that these posts would soon be ending, and everybody pretty much agreed that they had run their course.

"Like most things that suddenly show up in life in the midst of crisis, I know you will not be staying," Ada wrote. "Like Mary Poppins."

Yeah, that's who I always aspired to be — Mary Poppins. Wait till my buddies get hold of that.

"How life goes," Ada added philosophically. "And I know you already knew that."

Very sweet note, actually. Thank you, Ada.

Another reader said that readers check these posts each morning just to see if their names show up, like Romper Room.

That's a pretty apt comparison: Romper Room.

By the way, let me share this, from reader Kim Anton:

"Did anyone recommend Botanist Gin? My husband loves it. Also, strawberries are delicious right now, try a dollop of peanut butter on the strawberry, take a bite then spray copious amounts of whipped cream directly into your mouth."

Wow. Just ... wow.

At some point, I will transfer this daily love letter to a website, where I will post signups for the Gin & Tonic Society of Greater Los Angeles and the Happy Hour Hiking Club. Hope you'll come.

If you're unfamiliar with the Happy Hour Hiking Club, it's an underground group of L.A. misfits that hikes, then storms some local tavern that's not too nice.

One member described it as, "A drinking club with a hiking problem."

We meet monthly, except when we don't. The newly formed Gin & Tonic Society will meet monthly too. My pal/hero Hayes suggested the patio at Ashland Hill in Santa Monica.

Doubt they'd let us in. But I know someone who knows someone (the only problem-solving approach that ever works). So we have a shot.

If all goes well, we will donate a lime tree to Ashland Hill, and dub it the Giving Tree, and suggest anyone who ever needs a lime — or a moment of grace or a glass of icy gin — visit the Giving Tree at Ashland Hill.

Just to clear up a big misconception, I don't drink ALL THE TIME. It just seems that way. And I probably have every right, the things that have happened.

Even in the best of times, I'm wound like a ball of rubberbands.

But I'm not really brave enough to drink ALL THE TIME, for I know too well the complications that brings. Plus, I tire easily.

So I pick my spots. I drink to drink another day. Sometimes (gasp) I don't drink at all, for days or weeks at a time. My buddies need me, as does my son, as do my daughters, as does this pensive and needy wolf. With me, it's all about another day.

Just yesterday, the wolf-dog sprained her leg after tumbling at the park, yet another reminder of how capricious life is, how quickly it turns. Typical of a dog, she was deeply apologetic for having hurt herself so badly she needed to see the vet (she's fine).

But we keep on, don't we? Survival requires courage. There is also a madness to it too, a base frivolity, a sordid whimsy, and underneath it all, a wry and self-sustaining humor.

A splash of gin, a dollop of peanut butter ...

Here's to the weekend. Here's to you.

*POSH'S CHICKEN CHILI RECIPE
1 rotisserie chicken (or the equivalent)
1 onion
3 jars green salsa
1 tablsepoon cumin
2 tablespoons garlic
2 cups chicken stock
Sour cream

In a big pot, sauté 2 tablespoons of chopped garlic and a medium chopped onion in a splash of oil. Add the peeled meat from the chicken and three jars of Trader Joe's salsa verde — or some other green salsa available most places.

You slosh it around a while, maybe an hour, add a couple of cans of white cannellini beans and a tablespoon of cumin, a spice that tastes lousy till you add it to food. Oh, and a cup or two of chicken broth. Then slosh it around some more. Salt and pepper to taste.

Serve with a scoop of sour cream, a dash of hot sauce and a cold beer. Feeds six normal adults. Or about 60 Chardonnay Moms.

Loving The Lockdown?

Someone was noting the other day that he alternates between feelings of anger and sadness, which we can all relate to, I suppose. There is mirth within this situation too, and all sorts of little accomplishments.

The boy made iced tea on Sunday, for instance, and you'd think he'd freed the slaves of ancient Rome or solved the common cold.

He was euphoric over the iced tea, as he should've been. It was wonderful tea. Someone gifted us a bag of lemons — California is overrun with them now. So he sliced the lemons, poured the tea over a glass brimming with ice and sugar. It was a good day indeed.

There is time for this stuff now, like there never was before. There is time to brush the wolf and wash the car. If this keeps up, we're about a week away from making our own candles and gathering each night for Amish prayer.

It's a simple life, mundane and liturgical. A good day is when we pack a picnic, then go play catch in the park, just the two of us.

No question many moms and dads are secretly loving this lockdown. They are not scurrying home to rush through dinner, or jumping out of bed at the break of dawn to make a soccer tourney in San Bernardino. The rat-racy demands of modern life are on hold. Our nerves are better for it.

Alternating between mad and angry? Sure. But throw in the sweet tea of simple pleasures. We will never be the same after this, in some very significant ways.

This has been our long national timeout. I think Americans needed a timeout.

Hardly all good. For instance, it seems we've laid off all the bartenders. What kind of nation, in the turmoil of an awful crisis, lays off all its bartenders?

I mean, lay off the doctors, the cops, the governors, the president, but keep the bartenders and the hairdressers, the backbones of our great nation.

Maybe that's just my opinion, strong and stupid, as opinions often are these days.

Sunday, the snails ate all the mums, and the kid ate all the cookies.

Suppose you woke up in a Doris Day movie? That was Sunday.

"Doesn't she smell like lavender?" the boy asked after hugging the wolf good morning.

Honeysuckle, actually, not lavender. I went outside Sunday morning to find White Fang had chased something into the hedge, then twisted her leash around a landscape light, pulled down the big trellis of honeysuckle, dug up the dirt a little just for kicks.

She keeps chasing bumblebees through the flowerbeds. I scold her about not eating nature, but she insists.

One day, a bee will sting her in the esophagus, and I'll be the guy giving mouth-to-mouth to a full-grown Siberian wolf on the front lawn of a suburban home, the sprinklers kicking on at an inopportune time, mud and saliva flying everywhere, and rainbows in the sprinkler water.

The neighbors will spill out of their homes to watch and heckle us. We have a good neighborhood for that. Someone will probably pass a cheese plate.

"Please don't eat the bumblebees," I scold the wolf/dog.

She smelled very good, I won't lie, after attacking the hedge of honeysuckle.

"At first, I thought it was my own BO," the boy said when he hugged her.

For the record, the boy's natural musk does not smell at all like honeysuckle. It smells like anti-honeysuckle, the polar opposite of anything floral.

It was a warm weekend, a summery one. The sunscreen came out, the hats, the garden hose to wash the cars.

"Chicks don't really wash cars," my daughter Rapunzel reminded me as she washed the car, and missed more spots than she sponged.

So I guess I should be honored that she washed the car at all.

We broke the pod, by the way. We took one pod, my younger daughter's, and merged it with our pod, after going down the checklist to be sure each pod was safe:

"Who are you seeing?"

"No one."

"How do you feel?"

"Fine."

We hadn't hugged her in more than a month, not on her birthday, or that one day when the world seemed to be ending.

So she and her little brother caught up on their hugs, while I lay on the couch smiling. Things were kinda normal, for once. She'd brought her laundry, Swiss mountains of t-shirts and yoga pants, which I think was the real reason she came by, not to hug us. But as long as she was there ...

Then we made chicken, with Mexican street corn and a salad dressing the boy whipped up himself, using olive oil, salt, the fresh lemons someone left on the porch.

We sat on the patio and ate barbecued chicken. The day never cooled. It was summer. We had clean cars, and we had each other.

And, for a moment, it seemed everything might be all right.

Hooch In Your Coffee

As you've discovered, this is the little Happy Hour we now hold to start the day. Put a little honey in the tea, a little hooch in your coffee, some cream cheese on your bagel, whatever your pleasure. No one will know but me.

Honestly, I'm not much of a day drinker. Turns me into a cheerful chatterbox, and nobody likes that. Then I get drowsy about 4 p.m., cranky by 5.

So I'm not much of a day drinker, except for birthdays, holidays, tailgates, arcane European milestones, ballgames, anniversaries, picnics and pandemics. You get the idea. I try to pick my spots.

All I know is that the longer this crud goes on, the deeper I burrow into bed at night, as if zipping up my sleeping bag against the strange sounds coming from outside the tent.

I woke last night to the sound of the wolf panting. Really, it was like a bear eating marshmallows at the foot of my bed.

Pant, pant, pant.

I woke with a start. Whaaaat ... whooooo? Oh, it's you.

"Does she know something?" I thought. "Or did she just have a bad dream?"

Do pet wolves even dream? Do the dreams involve chipmunks, blue-plate specials and Hootie and the Blowfish?

In that case, the wolf is stealing my dreams, an awful thing to take from someone you love. Give me back my dreams, you idiot!!!

And quit your panting. If anyone needs to pant around here, it's me. May is moving in, warm as toast, then summer ... oh, gawd.

Lately, we've been taking the pensive wolf on long car rides, the boy and I, so we don't have to look at each other, we can study the road instead. Seriously, if my teen son goes much longer without a haircut, he will qualify as wildlife.

Anyway, we take a 30-minute ride almost every day to practice his driving, usually in the evening, as the day turns to cotton.

As we do, the wolf pokes her head out the window, squints into the breeze, and you see that gleeful smile, like winter sun, pass over her face, from one meridian to the next.

It is the most joyous I have ever seen our wolf. She has been through some traumatizing times. Then suddenly, this past March, we were all home 24/7.

"When does it end?" she must think. It's either the Golden Age for dogs or their worst nightmare.

To avoid expensive wolf therapy, we take her on these gentle car rides, where she pokes her head out the window to size up small dogs and their small owners. Yum.

It seems instinctual, dogs' passion for putting their heads into the wind. I suppose we should all taste the wind a little.

Pant, pant, pant.

That's not the only news I have to share this morning. Just yesterday, my old pal Nancy told me that I could add fresh lavender and thyme to my new best friend, gin.

Lavender is everywhere right now, it seems to be growing wild in the flowerbeds, in the lawn. But I know nothing of thyme, except that it's fleeting and you have to make the most of it.

And suddenly, there are roses everywhere too, have you noticed? Like weeds, these things. Red ones, pink ones, white ones in snowy drifts.

They smell kinda funny, but I guess I'll get used to it.

Amid all this, Coach Callahan just texted an old photo of our sons at opening day, back when they were 5, probably, and they wore their brand-new baseball pants cinched up around their armpits, and they didn't know quite where they were or why.

Now, they are 17, their pants still don't fit, nor do they know quite where they are or why.

But honestly. Does anyone?

Lavender In Your Lemonade

here's a hole in the flowers where a basketball plopped. I asked my son about it, and he said he knew nothing of the hole in the flowers or who might've done such a thing.

After six weeks in lockdown, my son and I have fallen into the gentle chiding of old chums, a shorthand of remembrances.

One day, as we were out practicing his driving in endless loops, I made him stop suddenly for one of those little book huts people put out, the ones that look like elaborate mailboxes. I needed a book. I always need a book.

"Stop!" I yelled, and he jumped, then pulled to the curb. I trotted back 50 feet to the hut and pulled out something, anything, a book, just any book.

Now, every time we pass that little hut, he shrugs, "So, need a book?"

So now, we have taken to teasing each other about idiosyncracies. What do you call that, other than friendship?

I told him I will be sad when he goes but not. I might even find a girlfriend, someone who likes to throw the football, or spend Friday nights watching Joe Pesci movies.

"People like that don't exist," he says.

"A boy can dream," I tell him.

A lot of the good women are married, and some of them are simply too young. I won't look at anyone born after 1965, for instance. "Why limit yourself?" you ask.

Because I like wine that's been in the bottle a while.

This is really just a flea market of survival tips, isn't it? Soothing words and recipes. Somewhat funny jokes.

Gentle humor is the best humor. It's like stirring the soup or taking bread from an oven — soothing in a way you don't quite understand.

Marshmallow stew was yesterday's little revelation. Some saw it as an actual stew, others saw it as a chocolate-marshmallow-nut dessert topping, served warm over vanilla ice cream, so that the ice cream melts a little on the edges and becomes extra satisfying in that soothing way you don't quite understand.

Evidently, life is full of tiny pleasures we don't quite understand. Like sucking the extra gin off ice cubes, that would be my equivalent. Through the icy glass, you see a room humming with laughter and friends.

How sweet will that evening be when it comes, sweeter than ever? Soon, all of life itself will be sweeter than ever … a big simmering marshmallow stew.

"It was the age of wisdom, it was the age of foolishness," is how Dickens put it almost 200 years ago. Maybe it is always that age.

When I think about it some more, what we've really established here is a cult. But a good cult. You never hear about the good ones, just the bad ones, in Texas or the jungles of Guyana.

Ours is based in the jungles of suburban Los Angeles, brimming now with roses, invaded by roses really, as we noted yesterday.

I have never seen such roses, or even noticed roses, really. They are God's creatures, far more alive than most flowers.

As you may know, I'm a practicing Deist, someone who believes God created everything, then just took a long snooze so we could figure things out on our own.

I mean, how else do you explain life lately?

But occasionally, with roses, with Christmas, with sunsets over the water, he sends us these missives.

And he also sends us gin.

Yesterday, someone suggested adding basil to the gin, and another person said that you can put lavender in your lemonade.

If there's one lifelong memory I'll take from all this, it will be that you can put lavender in your lemonade. Makes me think of summer in the Hamptons. Makes me think of pretty grandmas in faded denim, with silver hair and piercing eyes. God sends us those as well.

As I've mentioned, we live in a strange little house I acquired as part of a gambling debt. With two guys and a wolf, it's more of a fishing shack or honky-tonk than a real home. We take laundry right out of the dryer and wear it wrinkled. There is $427.27 in loose change in the couch. No one turns the pillows.

The daughters are gone now, so you'd think there would be all this extra room. Yet it's barely big enough for a pensive pet wolf and a growing boy, whose hair now brushes doorways when he passes beneath them.

It is a glorious thing, this stack of hair — a "pompadour," I think they used to call it, a hairstyle named for this mistress of a French king. That alone should worry us.

Just for kicks, his sister used a blow dryer to straighten it the other night. Like an anaconda, his long straight hair slithered around the living room, before coming to a coil in front of the back door. Just to be safe, we let it rest there.

The next day, the boy decided he didn't like straight hair after all and started playing with his hair the way teenagers always have. He watered it and raked it and thwacked it with a wooden spoon. Finally, it settled back into the wavy pompadour he loved.

Me, I have the same leaf pile of hair I had in my high school graduation photo, full of Midwestern humidity and possibly gum.

Look, they say there is broken glass in my soul. Maybe. But there is also this. There are smiles. There is us.

And now, there is also you, with your lavender lemonade and your gentle words. Each morning there is you.

Pies Are Life

I f you get up too early, you can make it to the farmers market before the lines start to form. They say the weekly market opens at 9, but it really opens any time the vendors have their berries and their eggs out, usually around 7.

You can get the nicest bunch of cut flowers for 5 bucks, and for 9, you can buy the kind of bouquet that young men give to young women in those first few weeks of dating, the kind that say: "I like you. This is serious and possibly life-changing. Look out!"

Remember those days? "I like you. I think of you all the time — when I go to the bathroom, when I butter the bread. I like you, though I don't really know you. What exactly are you hiding? Till I find out: Here, take these nice flowers."

Back in the day, I specialized in difficult women, and I bought flowers for difficult women all the time, especially Posh, whom I convinced myself really liked carnations, because at the time I really couldn't afford roses.

"Carnations are the superior flower," I would say, with the assurance of a young man who had no idea what he was talking about.

I am no longer young. I still have no idea what I am talking about. But I still deliver flowers. Look out!

Saturday, I took some to Lannie, the pretty Mormon mom who picked some stuff up at Trader Joe's for us, and to our neighbor Anita, who'd had an especially difficult week.

I dropped some to Raji next door, a nurse on the front lines of the Coronacaust, who was about to take the antibody test to see if she could donate plasma. Because, obviously, running the COVID unit wasn't enough.

Jeeeesh, these people. Even in the worst of times, there are these people who humble us.

I once took a bundle of farmers market flowers to John up the street, the widowed attorney who bakes my son and me pies all the time.

I know, there's a lot of strange in that one single sentence, but he bakes the most unbelievable apple pies, and from time to time, we'll hear a knock, and there'll be John with another warm pie and a half-gallon of vanilla ice cream starting to drip.

Pies are life, and we need them now more than ever. And honestly, you should taste these pies. They have, like, nectar in them, and maybe a splash of bourbon and some German chocolate cake. Before he brings them over, the Pope blesses them, and angels blow good thoughts across the crust.

They're pretty good pies, is what I'm saying.

I don't know how to reciprocate, so one time I had some extra flowers and I dumped some on his doorstep. My daughter Rapunzel got such a kick out of it when she heard: "Two old widower dudes exchanging pies and flowers!?"

"So what?" I'd say, but I could see her point.

It's the season of flowers. One reader called it a "super bloom of roses," a very apt description. I've never seen such roses, particularly the white ones, which look like six-foot drifts of snow.

But enough about flowers. How was your weekend? I announced my retirement from the *Times*, so there was that little wrinkle. No biggie. I celebrated with a burger and a brew. (Okay, two brews. No burger. Three brews, actually.)

Look, it's not like Beethoven giving up the piano. Words are cheap, and just everywhere. So it's really no big deal.

I hope now to overcome the slight jeweler's stoop I've developed from slaving over a hot keyboard all these years.

I won't miss the long drive to work or deciding where to go for lunch with colleagues. The answer was always: "Nowhere. There's nowhere to go for lunch."

Now, I'll always have a place to go for lunch. My kitchen is pretty functional, and once or twice a week, I'll venture out to some taqueria or hamburger stand, the greasier the better, leaning over my plate with my jeweler's stoop.

I will work on books and a couple of TV projects and perhaps a column now and then.

The columns are carnations, not roses. So what? Like the Chardonnay Moms in our little town, they look far better in clusters than alone. So I'll write a few columns. Like this one.

The Facebook comments are as good as the pieces themselves, probably better. And they create community. As we're all learning, community is more vital than we thought.

And the recipes. My latest favorite tip (from Mary): "Add some good sake to your lavender lemonade for a treat."

Marry me, Mary. I promise you a very unusual life.

I'll also devote some time to charities, such as the Gin & Tonic Society of Greater Los Angeles, a fraternal organization I just started with a sorceress in charge of recruitment.

I think the sorceress, a Hitchcock blond named Sam, is a strong selling point and will attract all sorts of investors curious about our start-up (and certainly Sam).

Like most start-ups, we have no idea what we're doing, but we give really funny presentations. When they are over, people just fling armloads of money everywhere in hopes of being a part of it. Please, please, please ... take our money, please.

There is no headquarters for the Gin & Tonic Society of Greater Los Angeles, or even gin, or even tonic. I've got a couple limes is all.

It's a start-up, remember? But we have potential. We have limes. Most of all, we have stubborn and resounding hope.

And you ... we have you. I mean, what else does a guy need?

Hell On
High Heels

have a wolf. She has white eyelashes. If that isn't freaky enough, she has teeth like a shark and is very, very smart. Too smart. She's also "the smartest person in the room," as they say, at least when I'm with her alone.

White Fang Erskine is her name, and each day, she wakes me, putting her snout on the edge of the bed and huffing a couple of times like an old horse. She bats her white eyelashes over those Dodger-blue eyes.

She's really quite stunning, and like a lot of stunning things, she is a total handful, almost too hot to touch, or even argue with. Yes, she is a handful. In time, you just marvel over that and adjust your life. Handfuls are miracles. They can change your life.

As I said yesterday, I specialize in difficult women, starting with my own mom. It's Mother's Day this weekend, so I can't help thinking of Mom, an important influence.

She was more French than Napoleon, and fancy like Audrey Hepburn. A tomboy too.

A good cook. A master mechanic, she could fix a mower. An amateur seamstress, she could hem a skirt.

See, she wasn't just any mom. Honestly, are any moms like any other moms?

She sang "Frère Jacques" on car trips, for Christ's sakes, that's how French she was.

Frère Jacques, Frère Jacques,
Dormez-vous? Dormez-vous?

She even walked the dog in high heels — her, not the dog. But if she could've put the dog in heels, I'm sure she would have. And maybe a light, little cashmere sweater.

My mom was hell on high heels. Sent me off to kindergarten when I was 3, the way fathers send difficult sons off to join the Marines. I didn't mind. I was 3. What else did I have to do?

Besides, I immediately fell for Kathy Kelley, an older woman, age 5. Unlike me, she was fully potty trained. Still is today, and I am still in love with her 60 years later.

See? Moms know best.

My mom once rode a mini-bike, that's the kind of mother she was. It was the age of mini-bikes, and the Wagner boys had brought their chattering minibikes over to the house, and my mom — the French showboat with a laugh like a tugboat — jumped aboard one of the minibikes, and off she went, not knowing where the brakes were.

That's how my mom lived her life. Full throttle, not knowing where the brakes were.

Once, she tried water skiing. When she fell, she didn't let go of the rope, and we just dragged her for about 10 seconds, like Aquaman underwater, till my dad finally said, "You know, I think she's still on."

It was as if we'd hooked a marlin.

So we stopped the boat, circled back around, saw something bobbing in the water. Mighta been Mom. Mighta been a muskrat. Her hair was plastered to her head in a way we'd never seen, and her swimsuit was sort of askew in troubling ways. We'd never seen her defeated quite like that.

You couldn't really tell Mom anything. But bravely, we gave her a very important life tip: When you fall off your water skis, it's generally a good idea to let go of the rope.

"I'll do it my way, you do it yours," she said. "Just give me the stupid rope."

I miss Mom, gone now almost 10 years. On Sunday, we'll celebrate Mother's Day, and I don't have many mothers in my life anymore.

But I had her a long time, the best mother ever. The one who never let go of the rope.

Readers Respond

Kim Seefeld

My mom died 10 years ago next week too. She was a pistol too! A Swede who grew up in France in the winters Sang Frere Jac in the car too! Wish I could tell her how much more I understand about the things she said and did that I was too young and know-it-ally to understand then. I hope my boys understand those things someday too. Here's to moms!

Steve Wolcott

Thanks, Chris. Wonderful tribute! Hopefully makes us think of our own amazing mothers. I so much admire tough Moms. My mother was under 5 foot and played the accordion, toured with Bob Hope in WWII at 18. Supported Dad playing in local nightclubs and early TV shows until he got his business started. Tough cookie.

Suzi Cannataro Levin

You are absolutely right! My mom was like no other mom, too! It's been 22 years for me but I will honor her this Mother's Day as if she were still here, just like I do every year! And I will never stop missing her like crazy! 🖤

Deanne Vandernoot
Laughing and teary all in one breath!
My mom was in the chorus of the first *Phantom of the Opera* and also
sang Frere Jacques and hummed to Mario Lanza.
Still picture her camping in heels!
Truly the best♥!
Thx as always for bringing these moments to these difficult times.

Marva Felchlin
When I read your writing, I am reminded of this quote from William
Blake's poetry "To see a World in a Grain of Sand
And a Heaven in a Wild Flower,
Hold Infinity in the palm of your hand
And Eternity in an hour."

Kathleen Ikola Kenna
I'd like a do-over with my mom. It really wasn't until she was gone
that I realized she'd had a pretty crappy life. I could have done much,
much more to make it better. 😖

Women Peak At 80

I like short sentences and tall drinks. Tall women too, but I like short women even better.

Mostly, I like them all, particularly when they have a certain amount of tenure. To me, women peak somewhere around 80 years of age, with the laugh lines and the twinkle.

I might be the minority here. But I am right. Older women rule. I'm looking for a tall or short one, about 85, with a little money. And the money isn't even all that important. As long as they have the laugh lines.

So here's to the all the Mormon moms, the Chardonnay Moms and our moms, yours and mine. Here's to my pal/heartthrob Angie Dickinson, who's a helluva woman and was an even better mom.

Mothers pull on the heartstrings. They have star power. We hear their voices our entire lives. Much of everything good we ever do, we do with Mom in mind.

So, as it turns out, we really like our moms. It's nearly unanimous. Big revelation, huh? That's like saying we really like peanut butter with chocolate, or gin with tonic.

Listen, the world can take away our sanity, our security, our jobs. It can never really take away our mothers, who gave us the first sense that everything will be all right.

And it will.

After two months, I sense that we are waking from our long national nap.

The stores and beaches are reopening, and I can't help but notice that the floral shops are too, just in time for a bouquet for mom. It's like God finally stepped in.

Some of the kids I coached are becoming moms. That's so bizarre to me, that these former second basemen are all breeding, creating — we can hope — future second basemen with similar skill sets.

Two of the girls I coached grew up to become doctors. One went to Harvard. All thrived. I wasn't really teaching them about softball or soccer. I was just teaching them how to get up when they tripped and fell rounding third.

"Get up, Caitlin! Get up!"

In fact, I had one softball team where all the girls were named Caitlin, which made taking roll at practice rather repetitive.

"Caitlin?"

"Here!"

"Caitlin?"

"Here!"

Even worse than that, I once had a t-ball team where all the boys were named Brandon or variations of Brandon. One was Braedon. Another was Brendon. Against the Blue Jays, I sent Braedon out to play second base, and half the dugout ran out with him.

"No! Braedon! Braedon!" I screamed. "Wait, which one of you is Braedon?"

They all raised their hands.

My mom would've made a great coach. Since she was French, she wouldn't have bothered learning any of the players' names, she would've just called them by their jersey numbers. But she had such charisma, such star power, that they would've felt honored that she had forgotten their names.

Lord help the umps, had my mother coached.

Mothers' voices are music, sometimes strings, sometimes rock n' roll. We will hear them always, when we flub something, or wallow in self-pity, or don't pick up our socks.

Indeed, a mom's voice was music. Calling you to dinner. Wishing you goodnight. But you never took her too lightly. She could pin you to the wall with her words. She kept you honest.

As I said yesterday, I have no moms left. Posh is gone. My mom is gone, all the grandmas. Yet, as one reader reminded me, I have a lot of she's in my life. Such as my daughters, my sisters, and all those beaming nieces, pretty as the prettiest horizon.

And on the horizon will be babies and grandchildren, and rich full lives.

Out of trauma and challenge come rich, full lives. Mothers taught us that.

If the world were right and we could get one more day with our moms ... or an hour ... or a phone call, where they'd ask: Are you still getting those headaches, dear? How'd Jessica do on her test?

Then you'd talk about the weather a little bit and the pork chops you were fixing for dinner.

Then there'd be a pause, and you'd awkwardly say your goodbyes, till the next year, when you'd get to chat with them once again.

In a just world, that's what Mother's Day would be like.

Actually, it kind of is.

Calvin & Hobbes

I rise early to see the way the moonlight is hitting the dog. She's a snow dog, white as a polar bear, and when the moon sends light across her face, she glows like diamonds in a glass of tonic water.

Then I pour some coffee, let her out, and start on these gothic morning monologues.

I claimed the other day that these columns are carnations. Really, they're just bouquets of cobwebs from a groggy father who doesn't sleep so well.

"You ponder life out loud," my buddy Stokes noted the other day.

Yeah, sorry about that.

My son was pondering life too yesterday, wondering why yogurt had expiration dates: "Isn't it by definition 'expired?' "

So I pitched that concept to a few friends, who agreed with me for once.

Another guy wondered the same thing about cheese: "Isn't it just mold?"

The more we live, the more we ponder. Eventually, we'll get to the bottom of things. Or not.

Meanwhile, my son and I go through life like Calvin and Hobbes, our hands in our pockets, wondering what life will be like in this new Plexiglas world we're about to enter.

We're not perfect, no way. But I've seen marriages worse than us, business partnerships and legendary folk duos. We're unfinished symphonies, especially him. We're really just Calvin and Hobbes, a cartoon couple, two idiots wandering the page, looking for the ice cream truck.

At 17, he wears t-shirts that look like the flags of corrupt South American dictatorships. After two months without a haircut, his head resembles a pile of dirty beach towels. Naturally, he likes the look and plans to keep it.

He is now taller than me, a fact he brings up nearly every morning. "Hey, look, Dad, I'm still taller than you. Would you look at that!"

"Shut up," I mumble.

Last week, in the middle of a phone conversation, his puberty returned (it comes, it goes). In mid-sentence, between the subject and the predicate, my son's voice dropped an octave and half, from piccolo to stand-up bass. Sounded like Elton John in "Benny and the Jets."

This change in him seems too significant to be purely coincidental. It might've been triggered by the full moon. Or the tides. Or the end of my column in the *Los Angeles Times*.

Thing is, now that puberty has returned, I can no longer play catch with my strapping son. He zings the ball, chin high, and it is still rising when it spanks my glove 90 feet away.

Ouch.

In turn, my throws to him are like dying quails, looping down toward his shoe laces.

"Good one, Dad," he says, as he scoops it out of the grass.

When he started out in baseball, he weighed four pounds. After games, I'd just put him in my pocket and drive home. Now, he could put me in his.

As his voice drops, mine grows raspier. For every muscle he adds, I lose one. I am like the aging portrait of Dorian Gray.

As with Dorian, it's a case of hedonism vs. vanity vs. time. Time is winning. Time always wins.

So, nope, Calvin and I don't have life figured out.
Why does yogurt come with expiration dates? Why don't dads?
Aren't they both, by definition, expired?
Just throw me the ball, kid.

sleepless
Nights

Like our friend Sandra, I sleep in segments. We both rise at 1, then again at 5 to witness the moonglow. It's like a football game with a halftime show. The last time I slept through the night was 1986, when I started getting into gambling and children.

Same thing, you say? Yeah, that's my point. Children are maybe life's ultimate gamble. And by 1986, I was "all in."

Sandra also says she meditates each morning before watching the news, but sometimes rushes it to see what fresh hell happened overnight.

Don't rush things, Sandra. Trust me, fresh hells will wait for you. Another ambush. Another "I-do-not-believe-this" moment.

But other things also await, joyful things, significant pleasures. Mother's Day for one.

Yesterday, we brought up the famed theologians Calvin and Hobbes, whom my son and I model ourselves after, in the way that Kobe followed Michael, or Matisse followed Signac.

Life follows certain equations, and Calvin and Hobbes were living proof of that, more alive than many people, free spirits in a world full of ambushes.

The first equation — and this is just me talking — is that the vast majority of people are decent, something along 90-10, or even 95-5, it varies by the day of the week. Say, if traffic is especially snarly, you have 90% of the people good, 10% lousy. If traffic is light, you have 95% good and 5% lousy. Like that.

We're seeing that equation now in everyday life, in the grocery stores, on the streets. Ninety-five percent of society is good and decent and thoughtful and kind. They will do the right thing when pressed. The rest we should just push off a cliff.

Similarly, 95% of life experiences are good, 5% bad. These are the equations. Like the circumference of a circle or the Pythagorean Theorem, it should be taught in churches, schools, playgrounds and board rooms.

Maybe it's generous. Maybe your experiences are different. But I'll stick with my 95-5 ratio on most days; 90-10 on the bad.

Yesterday, we also talked about expiration dates, and there is no expiration date on the 95-5 rule, except maybe during the Crusades, and I was just a kid then and don't remember them hardly at all.

Today, many stores around Los Angeles will reopen, some hiking trails too. It feels, perhaps, like we have made it over the hump, as if the worst of the storm has passed.

Sure, life is still all kinds of weird. The other day, I held a door for someone, but she hesitated. We were too close. Holding doors for strangers may be on hold a while. Like I said, weird.

Yet things are loosening up, folks are venturing out in new ways, in the nick of time. That this mini-milestone comes on Mother's Day weekend makes me all kinds of happy. After all, it's mothers who rule the world — not armies, not despots, not popes.

More than anyone, moms instill our values and work ethics. It's moms, really, who gave us the 95-5 rule. They train us how to treat other people, using their tongues like whips. "Don't you EVER talk to people that way, do you hear me? Do you?"

"Yes, Mom."

Seriously, if you ever see a showdown between a mother and a despot, take the mom, give the points.

And what gifts we give the moms as the world begins to open up. A ray of light, a sliver of hope.

Don't you hate the way Mom's right all the time?

Well, mostly.

So damn the distancing. Give her a hug. It's her day, after all, and you know what she wants more than anything in this world?

You. Just you.

Driveway Dinner Parties

'll confess right up front that I don't appreciate a soupy pork rib. I prefer a rib that resists a little.

A rib needs a certain amount of chewiness, is what I'm saying. A good rib needs to kiss you back.

Took a nice sampling of baby backs over to Santa Monica on Friday night, for a driveway party with the daughters, the niece, and their respective boyfriends. White Fang came along, snatched two ribs off of people's plates, the way pet wolves will, dismissive of protocol. The guests were nice about it; I was appalled.

"Young lady, that will probably be your last dinner party," I told White Fang on the way home. "Hope those ribs were worth it. Seriously."

Probably were.

Driveway dinner parties are starting to take place all over the city, with careful people, at careful distances, drinking careful wines. I took beer, of course, because that's still the best buzz of all. As I was telling Rapunzel's boyfriend, Alex, a Friday beer is the best beer of the week, even now, in this fractured work world.

"Especially now," he said.

We sat around, six of us in beach chairs, entertained by the mere sight of other people in close proximity. It quickly cooled, as Santa Monica will. The best AC will always be the kind that rolls off the ocean waves at 5 p.m. and produces, what Walt Whitman called, "the mystical, moist night air."

The lovely and patient older daughter served two amazing salads. By amazing, I mean really amazing, a word (like love) that we maybe throw around too much. This time I absolutely mean it. Amazing.

The first salad was a standard potato, of remarkable texture, enhanced by anchovies, which gave it the saltiness of the sea. The second, a cucumber-pepper-ricotta salad, would knock your freakin' head off.

"I made the ricotta myself," my daughter says.

Honestly, with these two salads, some wine, a pitcher of Negronis, and a cache of cold beer, you didn't really need a main course. But I'd brought smoked ribs, so we ate them anyway, mostly out of courtesy.

Everyone seemed glad we did. Rapunzel's boyfriend even shook my hand when we were done, a sign I guess that he's actually cleaned his hand of the gooey-wonderful ribs. Who cares? I mean, I've got a wolf snatching ribs off of plates and a teenage boy who is pushing my buttons just for the sport of it.

I'm tip-toeing that line between happy and ornery, because in a few minutes, I will have to drive home. I wanted another beer but decided against it.

All in all, a successful driveway dinner party. I highly recommend them. At 8 p.m., all the neighbors wailed on pots and pans and screamed out the windows in support of the frontliners. My legs got cold. Rapunzel told the story of how she got drunk one night and applied tanner to her own legs, leaving a cigar-colored splotch on her ankle that may last forever.

We talked about food a lot, and less about our work than usual. I confessed that I am always confusing ricotta for risotto, and when I say one, I might often mean the other. They are nothing alike, yet they seem cousins.

I also admitted that I didn't see the point of adding a teaspoon of anything, that I couldn't imagine how a mere teaspoon changed a dish in any appreciable way ... that to make a difference, you had to add, at the very least, a tablespoon, maybe more.

"If it's worth doing, it's worth overdoing," I said.

"How do you feel about nickels?" my niece's boyfriend asked.

"What's the point?" I asked, sticking to my guns.

The night grew long. The lovely and patient older daughter talked about how her mother never measured anything, and took liberties with recipes, substituting feta for blue cheese, to mixed results.

My daughter's fiancé, Finn, explained how he's going to turn their front yard into a backyard, with lounge chairs and tiki torches. Rapunzel talked some more about the paint job on her legs. Everybody raved about the smoked ribs when really it was the salads that were the stars.

Amid all this, I wondered how, on this Mother's Day weekend, we could honor the kids' late mama bear. Maybe I should make a teary toast? Maybe I should tell a funny story about the time she almost fell off a rental horse.

But really, they remembered her for me. Just by being there. Just by smiling and giggling the same way she once did.

That's how they told their mother's story. Amazing.

BBQ Lip Gloss

I n our last episode, I was juking the wolf in hopes of getting her to put down a baby back rib she'd stolen off someone's plate, during a Mother's Day dinner that was just how I like every social event: plain and simple.

I'm so sick of fuss. In L.A., fussy spectacle is a tradition. You see it in the restaurants, the parties, the stores. It frucks with our value systems, to be honest.

If nothing else, when this lockdown is over, maybe we can return to life's plain and simple pleasures.

Because L.A. nails those too. When you think of the best moments in Los Angeles, they usually involve beach walks and bonfires. And kids, of course. Damn kids: You love 'em. They leave you. You love 'em even more.

Anyway, that's my rant about fuss. If you couldn't tell, I don't care for it much at all. Yet look at me, making such a big fuss about fuss.

Certainly, though, this lockdown has recalibrated our priorities. For me, it'll be difficult to spend any time with the Kardashians after this, that awful world of pregnant excess.

As my friend Tonya said yesterday, after the rib episode, "Barbecue sauce makes the best lip gloss."

Sounds like an apron or a t-shirt.

By the way, I've declared an early start to summer. There. Done. Let summer begin.

Usually, Memorial Day is the kickoff point, but holidays are so compromised these days, and there will be no parades this year, no picnics on what is always one of my favorite weekends.

Last Memorial Day, they put me in a parade, at the very beginning, where my role was to assure people that the parade was about to get much better.

"Seriously, this really isn't even the parade," I told kids seated at the curb. "This is just the pre-parade. The good stuff is coming up. Incredible."

My buddy Charlie drove me and my son. We had a blast.

That's my latest summation for anything good. "We had a blast."

We had a blast at the driveway dinner party the other night, then Rapunzel came for dinner two nights later, and we had a blast again, with Korean short ribs and a big wok of noodles that looked like a country singer's wig.

The clear noodles blobbed from the bowl, as if a canister of gas had gone off, inflating them. To me, the best part of cooking is when something funny happens in the kitchen when lots of people are around.

Then we sat on the patio, lit some candles. It wasn't a big boozy thing, just a quiet dinner where we heard about the boyfriend's latest work project and made fun of my son's hair. Talk about blobs.

The next morning, I found an old bottle opener in one pocket of my shorts and some bottle caps in the other. That's when I concluded that summer had already started and decided we needed to acknowledge it.

Summer begins the moment you carry around an old bottle opener instead of car keys. Summer begins when you still have barbecue sauce in your cuticles on Monday morning.

Now, more and more, people are getting out for hikes and gathering responsibly for distanced rib fests in the yard. You can't crawl in a hole over this.

Remember, barbecue sauce makes the best lip gloss. If only I ran Revlon, right?

My dog-walking friend Karen said she hopes we
entirely to the way things used to be, that we realize :
grammed and time-twisted our lives had become.

My other dog-walking friend Nancy said she now dreads the
empty-nest feeling that she'll get when her daughter Anna goes back
to New York soon.

Empty-nesting is the heartbreak you feel when you think nothing can break your heart anymore. It is a measure of how much we
love our kids. Sometimes, it can be almost debilitating.

For many parents, the next few weeks will be: "Empty Nest: The
Sequel."

"You get the blessing of one of the lovely daughters returning
home during COVID and you get to know this daughter as the delightful adult she's become. A friend, a cohort, almost an equal," another pal wrote.

"And now, that I've come to love and appreciate this wonderful
adult and companion, she's off again to her next life. Without me to
protect her from the evils of life without a mask. Or ..."

Sigh. Damn kids. As I said: You love 'em. They leave you. You love
'em even more.

All I could do for my friend was to quote my favorite physician
(Dr. Seuss):

"Don't cry because it's over. Smile because it happened."

whiskered
wisdom

Dogpark Gary is my Aristotle, a man of rare wisdom. Do you have an Aristotle in your life?

Well, I'm not sharing Dogpark Gary, whom the wolf and I meet every weekday morning at the little park near the house.

Sometimes, it's like a conversation with a brilliant philosopher, other times a conversation with your favorite barkeep (same thing?).

Other times, it's like chatting with your cranky old man. If you loved your old man, you'd love Dogpark Gary.

Gary is brilliant about a lot of things: ribs, rubs, home repair, football. But mostly, he's an expert on how life used to be before things got so crazy that California hardly seems like California anymore — not so civil, not so sun-blessed.

The other day we talked about the kids missing proms and how sad that was.

Dogpark Gary recalled the enormous prom dresses of the late '50s and early '60s — almost antebellum hoop skirts — and how a guy could get lost in one of these prom dresses looking for his Peggy Sue.

"Hello in there ..."

You couldn't find the girl in all those layers, let alone the promised land. Those prom dresses were the best form of birth control you could ever imagine.

I talk about how my late wife didn't have brothers, which resulted in an idealized view of what men were really like. If a girl grows up with brothers, she understands men on an entirely different spectrum — the playfulness, the need to goof off a little. Having a brother is a crash course in what men are really like.

"So I'm not dating any woman without a brother," I concluded.

"You're not dating any woman period," he said.

"But when I do ..."

Dogpark Gary is 75. His wife had a birthday this week. "I told her I liked her better when she was 25."

"Were you married then?"

"No."

That changes everything, doesn't it? Lots of good things happen in a marriage: kids, careers, vacations. Lots of bad things happen too. Dogpark Gary and I are frank about both. And how there's a silver lining to almost anything.

"What's today?" I ask.

"I'm retired," he says. "Every day is Saturday."

Dogpark Gary stays active, yet he's in no hurry. He drives the speed limit in his old ragtop Jeep, and young drivers frequently honk and flick him off.

He shrugs. Big deal.

For 16 years, Gary climbed telephone poles and strung heavy lines in the rain and hot sun, working amid lethal levels of electricity.

Loved the work, the camaraderie, the physical challenges, till he wrenched his back and had to become a building inspector. Didn't like that so much ... the politics ... the grumbling of office workers.

But he prided himself on that work too, he says. He says he was fair and affable and thorough in his job-site inspections.

"I was only offered a bribe once," he said. "Three-hundred bucks in a Christmas card. I handed it right back.

"I wouldn't even have a cup of coffee with a contractor. That crossed the line. Then you became his pal."

What's the big deal? So an inspector and a contractor become pals?

Well, when work crews poured concrete foundations, Gary had to sign off that they did it properly, included the right reinforcing rods, that they followed the engineer's plans. If they didn't, that put lots of lives at risk, sometimes hundreds of lives, particularly here in earthquake country.

These days, Gary has a rescue pitbull named Jack. Lived on the streets. Just after he got him, Jack swallowed a tennis ball whole, like a cupcake, and Gary paid thousands of dollars to have it surgically removed. If not, the rescue pitbull would've died.

"Worst dog I ever had," he says. "But I'll keep him."

They are together always. If you spot Gary, you spot the dog, ambling down the boulevard in that old white Jeep, as the dog pokes his head out the passenger window gulping for air.

Gary leads a simple life, a life of integrity, in a little house, on the edge of Glendale. There are lots of Dogpark Garys in the world, yet at the same time, not quite enough.

He's also a reminder that we're never too old for role models. Or to reach out for advice.

Hope you've found someone in your life like Gary. If not, I hope you do. Don't the best people always have time for a chat?

And they'll be glad to remind you, in these troubled times, that this too shall pass.

These Damn Masks

I realized yesterday, on a quick little hike through San Pedro — perhaps the most underrated corner of Los Angeles — that we're going to have some pretty funky tans and sunburns this summer, what with the masks and all.

By the time I was done, I looked like Homer Simpson, the mask giving me his hound-dog 5 o'clock shadow. Wow, it's gonna be a weird summer. It's already been a weird year.

When does it stop? Is it 2021 yet?

These masks ... dear gawd, these masks. I pass out nearly every time I'm in the checkout line. My glasses steam, and I gulp like a goldfish.

Time for a little ocean air, which is what brings me to San Pedro, among other things. San Pedro is a paradise for knockabouts like me. Looked for whales, didn't see any, just a couple of surfers was all, slaloming through the rocks.

Yet there is the sun, the surf, the whispered lilt of the sea breeze. Such a sedative. If you bottled that, what would you have? A Valium-based bourbon? I wouldn't trade a walk along the bluffs at the Fermin Lighthouse for almost any drink or drug. It is a drink and drug.

Fermin Lighthouse is perched atop a storybook cottage. At first, you can't even tell it's a lighthouse. And it is surrounded by the biggest magnolias I've ever seen. It's like running across good friends at a bad party.

Get out to places like this when you can, in safe and sensible ways — I demand it. Mental health equals physical health, and there's no pop like the pop you get from looking down 200-foot bluffs onto a squadron of passing pelicans.

On Wednesday, no one was bumping shoulders, I didn't hear a cough or a sneeze or a wheeze or a woofle. And I left two hours later with my Homer Simpson tan and a vow not to let our shady indoor life turn me into a big bowl of yogurt.

In May, sunshine is an "essential service."

I don't know quite what to make of the extended lockdown. To me, it seems an overreaction, yet overreactions have served us fairly well so far.

There is an art to moving forward in difficult times. I find our local leaders both sensible and uninspiring. It's all kinds of ironic that, while thousands of California kids are taking their AP history tests, it appears that our mayor and governor have no idea who Churchill was.

As with AP tests, there are few easy answers.

At what point — in the sunny, sneeze-free days of late spring, do we loosen the reins and let people make a living again? Because that's vital too. Financial health equals mental health equals physical health. COVID is hugely contagious and only rarely lethal.

It is lethal, though, and heartbreaking losses mount. Our dear friend, Terese, the boy's fourth-grade teacher, lost her long fight with COVID two weeks ago.

Thank you for your prayers. We live in a world where evening prayers melt in the first light of dawn.

I have no answers, just a hundred million questions. The only thing I know for sure is that one of the absolute sweetest people on the planet is no longer here.

Why Terese and her big Greek heart? She was there for my son when he lost his mother. Now, two more kids are without their magnificent mother, the ultimate symbols of everything that we hold dear.

I mean, maybe God needed an assistant? Or someone just right to work with the kids?

Love you, Terese. You were our sunshine.

Breakfast Burritos!

I f you time it right, you can walk past our local Mexican joint at the exact moment they're burning off the grill, when bits of chorizo, bacon, pepper and onion season the air in a big greasy tornado.

Exquisite is too weak a word.

We pop in for a breakfast burrito now and then, just to get our fix. Breakfast burritos might be reason enough to live in Los Angeles.

There are other wonderful reasons, for L.A.'s a curious little place, full of surprises. But breakfast burritos are the best reason — big whoppin', ridiculous logs of joy. It's almost an ordinance that they be too big.

Indeed, breakfast burritos may be the only experience in America that still exceeds our expectations.

They are also the ultimate hangover cure. Soak up everything: toxins, pain, heartache, self-doubt. If a breakfast burrito doesn't make you feel better, order the morphine drip.

Hope has been a big topic lately. Loss of hope is the saddest thing. We've been robbed of so many friends and comforts lately. Hope you haven't lost hope.

This week, we found lots of reasons for hope, despite all that we face — the disappointing extension of the stay-at-home order, mixed with news that when COVID doubles back, it can be even worse.

The media usually fixates on the worse possible outcome. The rest of you have a better balance, thankfully.

This week, a vintage lighthouse lured us to San Pedro, where red foxes run the bluffs and the sea breezes sub for your first drink of the day.

In Santa Monica, we enjoyed a driveway dinner party, with salads by the lovely and patient older daughter that reassure us that life can still be full of festive surprise.

We mark all celebrations with food, and this was no different. Lately, with the weekends just like the weekdays, I've been trying to fix some special feast to make a Saturday or Sunday special. Last week, it was ribs. This week, it'll be ribs again. Next week? Why not ribs?

I think I may have ribs for the rest of my weekends. I always thought that you could open a successful restaurant that serves ribs almost exclusively, with baby backs, Korean short ribs, thick and meaty beef ribs, maybe even those incredible tomahawk steaks (I'm not sure if they are a rib or a steak, maybe both?).

I'd call the restaurant "Bones," and it would be the happiest place on earth, with picnic tables and checkered tablecloths and big icy buckets of beer. It'll be like a New England seafood shack. Instead of lobster, it would serve ribs and frame-worthy West Coast sunsets.

You'd also have the choice of two salads, the ones my daughter made and are listed below.

Hate to give away trade secrets, but one was actually borrowed from *Bon Appétit*, and the other is merely a traditional potato salad, with little twists of anchovies. Pure genius, my daughter. I mean, who thinks to put anchovies in potato salad, yet it is the one ingredient it's been missing for the past hundred years.

Ribs. Ricotta. Corn on the cob.

Perfect for our summery outpost by the sea — a raucous place called Bones, representing hope and resurrection.

Have a good weekend.

SALAD RECIPES

CHARRED PEPPERS, RICOTTA AND CUCUMBER
1/2 cup walnuts
6 tablespoons extra-virgin olive oil, divided, plus more for drizzling
4 sweet Italian frying peppers or Anaheim chiles
1 1/2 cups whole-milk ricotta
1 lemon
6 medium Persian cucumbers (about 1 pound), sliced on a deep diagonal
1 cup mint leaves, torn if large

Place a rack in upper third of oven; preheat to 350°. Spread out walnuts on a rimmed baking sheet and toast, tossing halfway through, until golden brown, 8-10 minutes. Let cool, then crush into large pieces with a flat-bottomed measuring cup or glass.

Meanwhile, heat 2 tablespoons of oil in a large skillet, preferably cast iron, over medium-high. Cook peppers, shaking pan and turning peppers occasionally, until skins are lightly charred and flesh is tender, 6-8 minutes. Transfer peppers to a cutting board and let cool slightly. If peppers are large, cut in half lengthwise.

Combine ricotta and 2 tablespoons of oil in a small bowl; finely grate zest from lemon over and mix well. Season lemon ricotta with salt. Set lemon aside.

Combine peppers, cucumbers, mint, and half of walnuts in a large bowl. Cut reserved lemon in half and squeeze juice into bowl. Drizzle in 2 tablespoons of oil, season with salt and toss to coat.

Transfer pepper mixture to a platter along with any juices in the bottom of bowl. Dollop lemon ricotta over and top with remaining walnuts. Drizzle with more oil and season with black pepper.

Recipe by Andy Baraghani, via *Bon Appétit*

OLD FASHION STYLE PICNIC POTATO SALAD
4 pounds potatoes — white or Yukon gold
1/2 cup mayo
1/3 cup white vinegar
1 teaspoon salt
1 teaspoon ground black pepper
1 teaspoon dijon mustard
2 tablespoons whole grain, old style mustard
1/4 teaspoon celery seed
6 oil-packed anchovy fillets, finely chopped then smashed with back
of a fork into a paste
1/3 cup red onion, finely chopped
2 hard-boiled eggs, halved and then sliced thinly
2 large dill pickle spears, chopped

Cook potatoes
Rinse and peel potatoes. Cut into large chunks — about 2-inch cubes/
pieces. Put in large pot and cover with cold water and salt generous-
ly, cover and bring to a boil. Remove top once they start to boil and
boil for about 10 minutes or until easily pierced with a fork. Drain
and set aside to cool.

Create dressing
While potatoes cook, whisk together mayo, vinegar, salt, pepper,
both mustards, celery seed and mashed anchovy fillets. Result will be
like a thin dressing, but it will thicken when poured over the starchy
potatoes and chilled.

Combine
Toss potatoes, dressing, red onion, hard-boiled eggs and chopped
pickle in a bowl and stir. Chill until ready to serve. Even better if
made the night before.

Serves 8-10
Time: 20-30 minutes plus time to chill

women shave?

I get the most interesting mail.

"Dear humorist," someone wrote over the weekend. "Did you know women shave their faces?"— signed, a woman.

No, ma'am. I did not know that. Tell me more ...

Come to think of it, tell me less. I find women's personal grooming to be kind of medieval.

Seriously, the things you do to impress men — and each other — can be a little gruesome. So be it. During the Coronacaust, I've come to terms with the fact that I can't control a lot in life.

Primarily: women.

Here we go, another week, and the whole thing has gone from a curious and major inconvenience to something more. I woke up worried last night, and I rarely wake up worried. The lack of smiles in our lives is a bummer, wears on you in strange ways, and the masks don't necessarily enhance conversation or social exchange.

I'm at the deli counter the other morning, screaming, "Turkey! Turkey! Pan-roasted turkey!" through my mask. The deli person nodded patiently and, in three minutes, came back with a pound-and-a-half of ham.

"Thank you," I said, and just moved on.

Some things are worth fighting, other times you just shrug, smile and move on. I probably really wanted ham anyway. Love ham.

The boy was grocery shopping with me, and he refused to touch the shopping cart, though he seemed to think it was okay for me to touch the shopping cart. I guess the old buffalo is of less value than the young buffalo. This is America, after all.

Besides, I find that trying to reason with a teenager is a complete waste of time for both of us. Better to just prod him with sharp sticks, herd him, kick him as you would a young and uncooperative calf.

He woke up late Sunday complaining that his new bedroom, the one he moved into a month ago, made him oversleep.

"I think the sandman, like, sprinkles extra dust in there," he said. "Sand?"

"Dust ... sand, whatever," my son said.

To our credit, my son and I have had only one squabble during this two-month quarantine, which isn't too bad for a couple who has mostly just had each other for entertainment, plus his lousy taste in reality television, plus the dog that might be a wolf, might be poltergeist.

But one fight? That's worth noting. The disagreement was over technology, naturally — I hate it, he worships it. One night, I couldn't get the Bluetooth to shut off, and the speaker blared just as he was trying to watch more lousy TV. You can't begin to imagine his frustration.

But we got past that and actually seem to be getting along better than ever, him growing a little taller every day, me a little more stooped.

I realized over the weekend that all the elastic in my body is now gone, any sense of snap to my muscles, any tension in the tendons. I can barely even jump.

That just happened over the weekend, as he gets taller, stronger, quicker and more fierce. Ultimately, we have nothing in common at all. Yet we get along — weirdly and with the underlying knowledge that we have no other choice.

That gnaws at you too, but what are you going to do, besides overeat and overdrink? As coping mechanisms go, they're better than most.

I also found, this weekend, a growing sense of hope amid the reopening of public life and the unfurling of a few Memorial Day flags.

The trails are open, the tennis courts, the car washes — dear gawd, the car washes are finally open! Hallelujah.

As you may know, L.A. has the most magnificent car washes in the world, enormous monsoons of automotive cleanliness that define this well-scrubbed city overall. Car washes might be L.A.'s greatest contributions to modern life.

When I saw that my favorite car wash had reopened, I wanted to race through it on foot with the wolf. I was a little leery of the giant shammy and what it might do to my neck. Plus, the wolf would pull and chew on it, and I'd never break her free, for once she chomps down on something — a slipper, a foot — forget about it.

But we'd sure be clean. Naked too, for that's how the wolf and I always bathe. But there'd be lots of foam, so don't worry if you are uncomfortable with partial nudity.

Bottom line about bottoms: "People look better with their clothes on."

That's what my physician, Dr. Steve, is always telling me.

"Even volleyball players?" I asked.

"Everybody," Dr. Steve said.

"What about Julianne Hough?"

"Everybody," my doctor said.

Dr. Steve also once told me that there are 47 sexual positions, when really I can only think of three. Or, if I've been drinking a little, maybe three and a half.

In closing, I see much hope in the reopening of L.A.'s incredible car washes — and the trails and the cheese shops — in the same way Emily Dickinson saw hope in the simple flight of a hummingbird. Dickinson once wrote:

"Hope" is the thing with feathers —
That perches in the soul ...

Whew! I knew I felt a breeze down there.

I Like A
Little Fuzz

I thought I told you I didn't want any more info on female face shaving.

Yet you insist, giving me tips on plucking, de-planing, chain-sawing, de-clawing and a bunch of other facial grooming techniques I don't understand.

To be honest, I like a woman with a little fuzz.

We also established yesterday that there are — at most — three sexual positions: standing, sitting and lying down. My doctor claims there are at least 44 more.

But that's how people get hurt. Besides, I think it's better to master just a few than to get all show-offy and throw out your back.

And, quite possibly, your front.

Anyway, this whole Facebook stuff has really started to work out for me. The comments are far more entertaining than my silly little essay. It's as if I pen the first act, you pen the second, and so on. As any writer will tell you, the second act is the hardest.

So thank you.

Most recently, folks related to my miscommunication at the deli counter. Deli counter communication was never easy to begin with, and now you have to mumble through a mask, which makes you sound like a bank robber.

I seem to bat about .500 at the deli counter, though I try to be explicit, repeat myself constantly, make eye contact, wink. I should maybe just hold up big cue cards. Turkey! Pepperjack cheese! Listen, whatever I get, I'm happy for.

You rock, deli counter people! I'd say that to your face, but you'd just misunderstand and hand me 16 pounds of liverwurst.

Doesn't help that the face masks hide our smiles. I suggested painting on a smile, but that would just look clown-creepy.

I also suggested sign language to indicate a smile, but what are you going to do, walk around smiling with your fingers? People would think I'm drunk, and I'm already drunk, at least in public. That's why I have my teenaged son driving me everywhere.

"Where to next, Dad?"

"I don't remember ... oh, pickles. Take me to the pickle mall!"

Thank God for teenagers, who are really just "people in progress," so they don't expect too much.

"Living with a teenager is like trying to nail Jell-O to a tree," my friend Rosemary said.

I think that's being generous, Rosemary. But hand me some nails.

You know, I dread the end of my newspaper column — no one walks away from a column. I did, and I sort of dread it, now that I hear via email that people were actually reading the damn stuff.

Had I known, I would've made it much better.

Look, what propels me along, what makes me think that my writing life might actually get even better, are your reactions to the posts.

I am seriously digging the back and forth, the smiles, the banter. Gives me hope, that word I keep using. And gratitude, the emotion we will come away with once this is over.

Hope and gratitude. They are better together than alone. Like gin and tonic. Like Sonny and Cher. Like you and me.

So onward we go. Honestly, I get so much wisdom from you. I hear it's raining frogs in Chicago but that Idaho is relatively nice and the fishing is good.

It rained here in Los Angeles yesterday, spring's last fling. Big drops the size of schnauzers went barreling down the downspout and tapped heavy on the roof, as if knocking to get in.

Once in a while, a dreary day is good, rinses the leaves, splatters the windows, teases the tulips. After the rain, the roses look like they've showered in Champagne.

Writers like dreary days because they live in the shadows anyway. And a rainy day reduces the temptation to go exercise, or some other ridiculous activity.

Readers have been asking me what the third act is — what's next when I exit the paper in two weeks. What do I know? I've been day-to-day for 30 years. It's a wonder I got a job in the first place, let alone kept it so long.

I keep waiting to dry up a little, but it seems that each day I have one more thing to say.

And this coronavirus ... almost biblical in how it's changing lives. I'm not sure there's some useful parable within it all, some course correction, some significant spiritual lesson we can lean on, as there often is in brilliant biblical stories.

As my friend Cindy said, you come out of all this either a monk, a chunk, a hunk or a drunk. It can only go one of four ways.

All we know for sure is that all this has generated new levels of hope and gratitude. On those two fuels alone, wars have been won.

Here's the other thing: As long as that little desk lamp is glowing in the corner window, it will mean I'm still in there writing away — a book, a blog, a letter to distant friends.

And waiting for you to write back.

A Toast
To Posh

Yesterday, we were showering things in Champagne: roses, my silly career, you guys — my 500 new writing partners.

For the love of gawd, this Facebook thing ...

My buddy Jay confessed yesterday to really taking to gin and tonics, not bathing in them or anything, but making them a huge part of his daily diet, as many of us now do. Vitamin C is so vital. And, as we know, alcohol is an important sanitizer.

Trust me: My liver is so sanitized right now.

I went to a spiritualist once — Okay, three times — and she told me that in an earlier life, I was a swizzle stick.

"In many ways, I still am," I told her.

Anyway, everything in moderation. You can squeeze a lot of lime into the glass, a quick splash of gin, and lots of tonic.

Or you can skip the gin entirely and still be holding a beautiful and seasonal drink. There is the spritz of sea mist to the tonic, and everyone looks better in the soft glow of ice cubes in a heavy glass. I declare gin and tonics to be the drink of the summer, or in some cases, a tonic and tonic, lots of ice, lots of lime.

Trust me. We'll drink through this together.

My dogpark pal (Dogpark Gary) was talking about his marriage the other day, telling me how it's been 50 years for him and his wife, Geri, and how when they were first married, they didn't have a dime, really nothing more than love and pizza.

"Then the pizza ran out," he said.

Dogpark Gary is a bit of a spiritualist himself. Kind of an angry, spitty spiritualist, but a spiritualist just the same.

He gets wound up over things, I talk him down. I get wound up over things, he talks me down. We are both angry, spitty spiritualists. But we have a lot of laughs.

One of the things that really frosts Dogpark Gary is when servers in restaurants respond "no problem" instead of the traditional "you're welcome." You may as well throw darts at Gary's face than respond with a "no problem."

"You have a point," I tell him.

"Thank you," he says.

"No problem," I tell him.

With good friends, it's okay to push a few buttons, to tease them about their behavior and idiosyncrasies.

Me, I have no idiosyncrasies.

In fact, I'm damn near perfect, though not that bright. I had three kids before I realized what caused them: beer and early bedtimes.

In my defense, my late wife, Posh, was some sort of fertility goddess, gorgeous with a halo of chestnut hair, a size zero chassis and a sea mist smile. When she walked into a restaurant, other men would stand and applaud.

That explains the early bedtimes, I guess.

"Guess what," she used to say all the time.

"What?"

"I'm pregnant again."

"No problem," I'd say.

Yet it was a problem. Like Dogpark Gary, we had nothing more than love and pizza. Then the pizza ran out.

As I say, Posh was a fertility goddess. Some sort of Cone of Fertility hung over the house like a bad weather system. Posh and I had hardly touched in three years when she got pregnant with the fourth, the child we called "Baby Oops."

Stop me if I already told you this. But the other kids were older at that point, 11, 17, 19. They were so repulsed by the news of a new baby, and the hint that their parents were still physically intimate, that they got physically ill. They spit up and stuff. Two of them fainted.

"I'm sorry," I told Posh.

"About what?"

"The pregnancy," I said.

"You weren't even there," she teased.

Friday would've been our 38th anniversary. We were married in a hot little Lutheran church on the southeast coast of Florida, in mid-May, when the heat index topped 11,000. It was like those old movies where all the men are sweating through their suits and wiping their faces with white handkerchiefs, as if in surrender.

She walked into the church like a bowl of cherries. At the reception later, I remember how when we passed through the lobby, an older woman elbowed her husband.

"Huh, what?" the old man said

"See that?" she said. "See that beautiful bride?"

Happy anniversary, baby.

California's Jutty Broken Jaw

My penpal Ted, a *Times* subscriber since 1964, worries that the world is getting more miserable and less delightful.

"True dat," as the kids say, though I sense the world will make a comeback, rally in the fourth quarter, like at Lambeau, when the game is on the line, and the crowd is clapping in their hunting gloves.

This is hardly the Dark Ages, or even World War II. After a couple of cruddy months, we're on the road to a slow recovery, a vaccine and better times.

In fact, when I rise at 5 a.m., a ridiculous hour for anything except writing and letting the dog out, the sun is already starting to rise.

The light at the end of a very long tunnel?

I predict that by the solstice, June 20 this year, this pandemic will no longer taint our every thought. By summer, we will be living a little.

Lived a little yesterday, in fact. I decided recently that I would revisit some hidden gem once a week — my midweek church. Last week, the fetching harbor town of San Pedro. This week, Palos Verdes Estates.

With traffic still so light, it is now possible to get from the foothills to the sea in about 30 seconds. Suddenly, places you shunned for decades are extending a tanned hand.

As you know, Palos Verdes Estates is where you go when you want to see some bluffs. PVE is California's jutty broken jaw. The waves smash it every day. With its misty hi-res panoramas, it reminds me of Big Sur or North County.

Malibu is similar and spectacular. But Palos Verdes is greener, less blanched, and a better blend of land and sea.

PVE is L.A.'s best unbeaten path, and a rustic reminder of why we're here in the first place.

We lingered in the midday light. Fred Rogers is famous for saying, in times of distress, to "Look for the helpers. You will always find people who are helping."

I say, look for the light — the warmth, the sun, the stars and especially the sparkling smile of the thrashing sea.

Oceans like this have carried troubled souls to better places for thousands of years, literally and otherwise.

I see something inherently hopeful in the Pacific — an eternal Irish wink.

Or maybe, the light at the end of a very long tunnel.

So Long, Salad Bars

'm drawing a bead on a joint called Nelson's at Terranea, a luxe resort I've always heard a lot about but never visited. The southern reaches of the South Bay are like finding a fistful of sapphires in your pocket.

From the picture, Nelson's looks fine, kind of beachy and casual. Doesn't have that lived-in look that I prefer, a few nicks in all that blond woodwork, maybe a dart board on the wall. But this is Palos Verdes, not San Pedro. As you can tell, I am slowly making my way up the shoreline.

A coast crawl.

Palos Verdes is the kind of place hummingbirds go to retire. There are wild peacocks in these parts too; it's sort of famous for the annoying little pests, which can roost on your roof and create all sorts of havoc. But they're beautiful, so they get away with it, the way beautiful creatures often do.

Odd how the hummingbirds seem way smarter than their much larger cousins.

In any case, the California coast seems to exist in some sort of candied movie light, filtered through sea mist and butterscotch rays.

So I'm working my way up this coast. I'm thinking Hermosa might be next, or I might jump ahead all the way to Malibu, where I'm hearing about a burrito place that can change your life.

California can change your life. It's sure changed mine.

I'm glad to be here in what we hope and pray are the waning days of the pandemic. Could be, right? Not out of the question. Every day, there seems a bit of better news.

Still, there are concerns. The other day, I went to mail a letter. Should I lick the envelope? Should I open the mail without gloves?

Simple kisses are now forbidden, and Lord help salad bars; we won't see those for a very long while.

I've always been a sucker for a good salad bar. I like the beets and the shredded egg. I like the way the bowls of dressing separate just a little.

My dad could work a salad bar, a Picasso with tongs.

To him, it seemed a bargain, particularly if you piled the plate just so, with the heavy stuff on the bottom and a wisp of lettuce on top. He used to blend the various dressings — a little blue cheese, a little Thousand, maybe some French. It was a gloppy spectacle by the time he was done, a parade float, defeating the purpose of salad as a light pre-meal.

He may as well have ordered a complete steer.

Funny the things you think about. Did you ever imagine, in a billion years, that salad bars would go away or that licking an envelope would give you pause?

On Sunday, I'm taking the kids out on a pal's boat. Only thing better than having a boat? Having a pal with a boat.

Once at sea, we'll scan the horizon, for that's where you always look first, out toward the magnificent sea. Then we'll admire the coast, from PVE to Point Dume.

On one end, the bluffs I just visited. On the other, the Malibu burrito I've heard so much about.

Kind of a nice place we live.

You know, the peacocks can be ornery, but the people are pretty nice.

And the views?

Healing.

L.A. And Me

I am a sucker for the simpler things ... cool night air and the old fishing lures my grandpa gave me. It's no wonder I landed in L.A.

That's a tiny joke, for Los Angeles is a blowsy big city of enormous spectacle. We're an odd couple, to be sure. That L.A. won me over is one of the biggest plot twists of my life. But I like plot twists, and that's why I like Los Angeles.

L.A. is a thick and amazing book.

Sure, it's had a lot of work. Its beautiful women (and men) deem themselves not beautiful enough, and they blow up their lips, their eyes, their tushes, as if with helium, till they look like foil balloons.

Los Angeles shuns old age like nowhere else, tears down buildings instead of merely repainting them, seems to take pride even in cutting down old trees.

Yet it is also home to some of the finest, oldest sports stadiums in the country, and the elegant Hollywood Bowl. Go figure.

The Bowl will be closed this summer, as will Dodger Stadium, another landmark. I'm hoping that what Governor Hair Product says is true and that we can start having games soon, even if it's without fans at first.

Eventually, you have to punch back at the challenges life throws you, and seeing games again — even on TV — would be a rallying point for many of us. It hardly seems a holiday, let alone a weekend, without games.

The other evening, a friend of a friend was saying how sports define American seasons. She is from another country, with only one sport. But here in the U.S., she said, spring is basketball, summer is baseball, fall is football, winter is Christmas (not a sport, but we celebrate as if it's one).

I confess that, without hockey playoffs and spring baseball, I sometimes forget what season it is. Right now, I'd give 100 bucks just to hear the soft murmur of the crowd between innings.

Fall will be the big test. Autumn is our Festivus, the secular holiday we all can celebrate. It's vital, I think, that we have football again, our great national bonfire. You will witness a very glum and beaten-down nation if we don't have football to worship on bright October days.

And I wish there were weddings too, another seasonal sport. In particular, I wish there were my older daughter's wedding, which she micro-planned, then postponed, then postponed again, like many young brides.

Yep, there were tears. Even the wolf and I misted a little.

The other day, her sister pointed out the place where they'd rehearsed her wedding day makeup, something I never knew brides even did.

"As if she needs makeup," I thought to myself.

Now, the wedding is set for next summer, and I think that is for the best. It will be held in a grand old church they somehow forgot to tear down.

"Now are the woods all black, but still the sky is blue," Proust said.

In L.A., the sky is almost always blue.

And next summer, on her wedding day, the sky will be Dodger blue, blue as the sea, the bluest blue in God's paint bucket.

A Day on A Boat

The songbirds won't shut up.

It's unclear whether they wake me, or I wake them, but they're kind of chirpy, kind of sarcastic, as befits our house.

They're chattering away at 5:22, just after the sun comes up. Tomorrow, it will be 5:15. Each day, the sun rises a little earlier, and so do the songbirds. Then so do I.

"Darkness sticks to everything," the poet Tom Hennen said. Well, lately, yeah. But as we said last week, life gets better when you make a point of following the light.

As promised, we made our way to the sunny ocean the other day. My summer gift to my children, my gift to myself, was a three-hour ride aboard the Buen Camino in the tinseled late hours of Sunday afternoon.

We'd had a week. Slept funny on my left shoulder one night, and the curse of being single is you have no one to complain to about such things, no one to rub your achy shoulder and ask, "Is that better, should I make us coffee now?"

As you might guess, I've been working relentlessly to come up with a vaccine in my own kitchen. One morning, on the verge of a real breakthrough, I set fire to the sink.

So it feels as though we're making significant progress. Give me a couple more weeks.

Ideally, the vaccine will involve gin, tonic, lime, rye, vodka or cheaper brands of beer, because I have vast quantities of those. Gotta confess, a super icy gin and tonic might not cure anything, but it's the best placebo I've ever found. You simply feel better.

Take two and call me in the morning.

Anyway, the boat ride was a grand gesture, prompted mostly by the year's delay in my daughter's wedding. We needed to get out of the house, out of our heads, out of this mad cycle of bad news, and out on Santa Monica Bay.

Life is better on a boat.

Rapunzel brought sandwiches from Bay Cities, which after the Pacific Ocean, is Santa Monica's greatest single achievement. There are no words for their biggest hit, the Godmother; it's not the bread, or the motor-oil dressing, or the meats, which are just right.

It is all of it — not a single wrong quality and so many qualities that are just right. Like a memorable movie. Like Brahms.

And there on the boat, waving our sandwiches at each other, we celebrated.

We weren't sure what we were celebrating exactly, except that we were all together, and like the Godmother sandwich, we are greater than the sum of our parts. My daughters were there, my niece, their boyfriends, my son, all of whom we quarantined with.

I'd intentionally undersold this voyage, not building it up too much, so that when they stepped aboard Bill Austin's elegant old trawler, teak trim everywhere, there'd be a sense of surprise.

I am a sucker for surprise. I am a sucker, as I said yesterday, for the simpler things ... bird song, Jason Mraz, Miles Davis and the smiles of my children.

Maybe it's the totality of their ortho work I'm proud of, which came to about 17 grand, if I remember correctly.

Or maybe it's because I am one parent — an only parent — but inside me beat the hearts of two.

At one point, we were joined by a pair of dolphins. They torpedoed ahead of us, just in front of the bow of the boat, as if playfully guiding us through Santa Monica Bay.

Indeed, like the poet said, darkness may stick to everything.

Yet it's the summer light that we remember.

Prosecco In The Plants

've been pouring the leftover Prosecco on the plants in the front flowerbed, and they have never performed better. The fuchsia and the lavender seem happier. The small purple flowers, the ones where the boy's basketball always seems to plop, are springing gamely back to life.

Even the bumblebees have a nice buzz. Listen, if you have some flat wine in the fridge, and a lot of us do, I highly recommend it.

As I always say: "Wine flies when you're having fun."

Likewise, I pour my flat, leftover gin and tonics on the potted plants on the kitchen sill, and they are behaving better as well. Pretty sure alcohol is summer's not-so-secret ingredient.

It is warmer now, and that always makes me a little crazed, like a mad Danish prince in flip-flops.

This time of year, you could lose 5 pounds just washing the car. That would be a good thing, probably. We've fetishized desserts, my son and I, as we spoon old episodes of "Seinfeld" every night.

"Do you date immature men?" Jerry asks a woman he's met.

"Almost exclusively," she says.

When I blurt out the line before the actress does, my son looks at me like I'm some sort of sage. But I've seen this episode about 15 times. The way some men focus on Civil War reenactments, that's the way I focus on old episodes of "Seinfeld." In many ways, it is our greatest show.

There is more sociology and psychology in a single season of "Seinfeld" than there is in most college textbooks.

I mix things up though. I'm also currently reading a friend's manuscript about a frisky female private eye, and I have another novel going about a bachelorette party that goes horribly awry.

You know those people who juggle two drinks at once? That's me with books, always reading more than one at a time, when really I only have time for one.

No wonder I feel like an exasperated Danish prince, watering the plants with Prosecco and feeding bison to the wolf.

Yeah, bison. Dogpark Gary talked me into it, told me his pitbull really likes bison mixed in with his kibble. Suddenly, I've become one of those people who is spoiling his dog, now that the children are mostly grown.

As if I have an obligation to make everyone happy.

I've got to get over that. All of my own instincts relate to keeping my kids happy, or my pals, who are more demanding, or now this wolf, a total diva. Trust me, I know a diva when I see one.

I think I will start dating soon, probably L.A. divas, which will probably make no one happy. As Seinfeld says, first dates are like one long job interview, no one likes them.

And where would you take a diva these days? Down to the river to watch the possums play? Would you wear masks the entire time? If you kissed her good night, would you gently bump the fabric of your N95 masks? Magic!

Wonder if, under the mask, she had a mustache?

I stumbled across something Garrison Keillor posted the other morning. It was a passage by the poet Donald Hall about his life with Jane Kenyon, also a poet:

"We got up early in the morning. I brought Jane coffee in bed. She walked the dog as I started writing, then climbed the stairs to work at her own desk on her own poems. We had lunch. We lay down together. We rose and worked at secondary things.

"I read aloud to Jane; we played scoreless ping-pong; we read the mail; we worked again. We ate supper, talked, read books sitting across from each other in the living room, and went to sleep. If we were lucky the phone didn't ring all day."

That sounds almost perfect. If it were me, I'd throw in a game of naked Twister every once in a while. Or hit golf balls off the roof toward the homes of neighbors I don't like. I'd pour her a pint of cognac and read "Goodnight Moon" in the bathtub.

Obviously, I'm a little more playful than Mr. Hall. I like to stir things up a bit.

The other day, I had this thought: If I date again, the primary requirement won't be that she's a diva, or funny, or beautiful or a brilliant conversationalist, with abs like a banjo and ready to attempt the 3.5 sexual positions that I know.

The primary requirement will be that she can pitch batting practice to my kid.

I'm looking for a lefty with good control, who can throw 50 pitches, mostly strikes, and get breaking stuff over the plate.

"Do you date immature men?" I'll ask.

"Almost exclusively," she'll say.

If she throws a good change-up, I might marry her.

Whacking At stuff with Golf clubs

O n my last day of work after 30 years, I rose at 5 a.m., made my usual cup of coffee, splashed some kibble in a bowl for the wolf.

I fired up my computer. On my desk was a blossom my son knocked off the magnolia tree with a 9-iron he found in the garage.

I suspect that a lot of the great florists work this way.

"I couldn't reach it," he explained. "So I just whacked it with the club."

"Thanks, Tiger."

All at once it was an act of violence and an act of charity. He put it in a small vase and placed it on my desk.

Smells like Gilligan's Island.

It gives me peace, just the thought of him out in the yard, whacking it with that golf club. And my son didn't just dump it on my desk, he sought out just the right vase, added water, plopped the flower in it.

"Here, Dad."

He knew it was a special day ... my retirement day. From here on out, I would never have to spend hours on a freeway, then arrive home grumpy and hunched, the way working people do.

He was happy for me; he was happy for himself; he was happy for the freeways.

Honestly, the hardest part of leaving a big company after 30 years is getting your phone to go with you. In particular, I wanted to keep my number, and for 100 bucks, I could also take the phone. Since I was dealing directly with a phone company, you'd think they'd know the drill.

It was like a customer-service blooper reel: Three days, 12 phones calls, talking to this rep and that, barely able to understand some of them, and I'm still not certain this phone transfer will actually work.

I hate tech. And somehow technology senses that I hate it and takes its retribution.

I dread what technology will be like in 10 years. Will I be able to manage a plane ride? By then, how many passwords will I have? A thousand? A trillion? When I sign into my bank account, will they first scan my soul?

If I need a cab, will I just blink three times?

For the love of God, this stuff.

It's so Orwellian, you have to laugh. There are good things about all this though. I never stand in bank lines anymore. I can book a blood test. I can find my way anywhere, anytime.

I especially like that we can keep in touch. As one Facebook friend said, imagine what the last month or two would've been like if we hadn't had our devices to bring us together.

I used to mock Facebook. Now I sort of like it. But, ultimately, it's not the technology I like, it's you — your quirks, your humor, your tips on backyard barbecues.

I think the takeaway is that humanity will always blast through the walls life puts up for us, whether it's oppressive governments or oppressive technology.

For over two months, I've been posting five days a week, and I feel a bit like the young actor in the Stravinsky ballet who dances herself to death.

Starting next week, I'll dial it back a little. I'll be the better for it. You'll be the better for it. This way, we can keep the dance going a long time.

Please note the beautiful website my daughter created (chriserskineLA.com), with signups for the Gin & Tonic Society of Greater Los Angeles, an important organization whose work is just beginning.

You can also sign up for the Happy Hour Hiking Club — "a drinking club with a hiking problem" — or find past Facebook posts you might've missed.

See, isn't tech wonderful?!

Okay, that's going a little far. But if you seek out the blossoms and whack them with a golf club, you can produce a flower in a small vase that reminds you of Maui.

Have a drink. Have a weekend.

We'll talk soon.

Troubled Times, Troubled Minds

think retirement has really sharpened my focus and moistened my quill.

After two days, I seem more tuned in, and I've taken to jotting down tons of ideas on legal pads. Not good ideas. Mostly bad ideas, and plenty of them. Enough to keep me busy anyway.

"No work, no jerks, no problem!" said one retirement card, though in fairness, most of my colleagues were wonderful, with only a sprinkling of total jerks.

Great timing though, huh? Can't get a haircut. Can't get a drink.

In addition to COVID, there is now some sort of zombie apocalypse taking place each night, just after "Wheel" ends.

Troubled times, troubled minds. As an expert in troubled minds, I have a few thoughts:

Lots of people are sleeping poorly, waking at odd hours and unable to fall back to sleep. What's that about?

As your self-appointed shrink, I'm wondering what you think that's accomplishing really, other than making yourself cranky the entire next day.

Here's my offer: I'll stop sleeping poorly if you'll stop sleeping poorly. Seriously. You go first. Okay, I'll go.

Me, I haven't had a full night's sleep since the Chicago Bears won the Super Bowl in 1986. I just don't want that feeling to end. Subconsciously, I'm afraid it's all a dream.

Waking up would be such a nightmare.

To be a sports fan is to dismiss logic as a guiding principle in your life. But faith can get you through so much. Pick your savior: Jesus, Bruce Springsteen, single malt Scotch.

My own fitful nights ruin everything the next day, from feeding the chickens to doing laundry.

The other morning, I washed the sheets, and when I put the sheets back on the bed, they were still a little damp.

"Awww, screw it," I said, and turned on the ceiling fan.

I determined right then that I don't need a wife so much as I need a mommy. Prospective wife/mommies should not be scared off by this. You should be glad I'm being so candid. It'll save us a lot of money on therapists and attorney fees.

Life tip: You can tell a lot about a single man by the way he washes the sheets each month or two. For instance, if when I'm done, I discover a sock under the fitted sheet, I just usually leave it. I mean, who minds a minor bulge?

My advice when it comes to marriage: Don't marry a guy till you've seen the way he deals with damp sheets on his own bed.

Back to our national insomnia for a moment:

When I can't sleep, I try to think soothing thoughts of Katharine Ross in "Butch Cassidy and the Sundance Kid." If that doesn't work, I think of the snow sports — nude tobogganing being my favorite, though drinking cognac in seedy Sierra ski resorts is right up there too.

If that doesn't work, I go to the kitchen to work on the vaccine I've been cooking up. Making big strides there. Turns out, my vaccine is a gin-based solution, with little globs of honeycomb I bought at the farmers market, which is where I get most of my lab supplies.

"How do you use this?" I asked, holding up the honeycomb.

"You can smear it on a cracker," the bee lady said. "Or put a little wedge of it in a martini."

"Wait, did you just say ... martini?"

I'm biased, sure, but an icy glass of gin, with a bit of honeycomb twirling in it, is kind of a mitzvah. Even if it's not a total cure, by the third drink, who cares?

Isn't science important? See what we have to look forward to?

Keep in mind that I'm an odd little man of Victorian values who sings his pet wolf to sleep each night.

Yet this I'm sure of: Before this is over, we're facing a few more anxious bedtimes.

But aren't the mornings beautiful?

Happy Juice, Happy Friends

Definition of irony: My son is ranting about how schools should open full bore in the fall — the big COVID threat is over, he says. And in the midst of his rant, I cough a little. Just an abrupt clearing of the throat, but a symbolic cough just the same.

"Are you kidding me?" he asks.

"I'd never kid a kid," I tell him.

The cough was genuine, probably caused by a furball. The wolf is shedding her seven winter coats — huskies dress in layers. So White Fang's fluff fills the air like puffs of Sierra snow, landing on the couch, along the baseboard, and now apparently clogging my esophagus.

Cough, cough.

Bartender!!!

By the way, I mighta had a little too much happy juice the other night, as we celebrated yet another baby step toward normalcy.

"To the power of positive drinking!" I said in a Viking toast.

"Hear! Hear!" my buddy Bittner roared.

Like many people, we've started socializing a bit, the boy and I. We go to a nearby park and circle up lawn chairs at safe distances, curling our bare toes in the freshly mowed grass.

On my last day of work, we prayer-circled some chairs in the driveway, 10 of us. We never got around to the prayers, but the spirit of the Lord was with us. Or someone just like the Lord.

"Oh sweet Jesus ..." my daughters muttered whenever another loud buddy showed up.

The greatest part? Adult conversation. It was just nice to hear good banter again, the din of too many people talking at once.

I looked around and there were 10 different conversations going, nobody listening. We were like a tree full of birds, all singing at once.

So great to be out again.

The other night was similar. We gathered in Gary's backyard with Bittner and their beautiful daughters. Someone brought pizza. Cauliflower pizza. Cauliflower.

This cauliflower pizza was pretty good though. The sauce was just how I like it — dark as cabernet and laced with garlic. I closed my eyes, took a wary bite, followed by a big slug of gin.

"Wow, pretty good," I admitted.

"Isn't it?" someone said.

"I was talking about the gin," I said.

As you know, I'm not much for change, or even progress in general. One reader said the other day that she appreciated my "sarcastic warmth," which is really more of a broiling skepticism and throbbing mistrust. But call it what you want. Warmth is warmth.

Yet so much of life goes right by me. Really apparent things, things that everyone else seems to get. Cribbage. Geometry. Line dancing.

For instance, my buddy Sam reminded me Wednesday that June 3 was an important day in American history — the day that Billie Joe McAllister jumped off the Tallahatchie Bridge.

"Or was she pushed?" I tweeted. "We'll never really know."

Welp, Billie Joe was a dude, as everybody remembers except probably me. Duh.

"It was the third of June, another sleepy, dusty Delta day ..."

All I remember for sure is that he/she tossed something off the damn bridge. And that "nuthin' any good ever happens up on Choctaw Ridge." Which probably means I'll end up living there one day, on Choctaw Ridge. As I've noted, I specialize in difficult women and difficult places. Maybe Bobbie Gentry can move in.

In any case, we had a wonderful time in Gary's backyard, chomping pizza and "inhaling the smoky night," to borrow from the poet Dorianne Laux.

Lots to talk about. One moment everything is so rosy, the next so bleak. But the stock market was soaring, even Boeing. The moon came up over Gary's house like a big bowl of milk.

Then an earthquake hit, a minor quiver, a rim shot, centered 20 miles away.

I thought to myself: "The devil ain't done," then glanced over at that cauliflower pizza.

"Nope, the devil ain't done."

So I poured myself a little more happy juice. In a few minutes, everything seemed gauzy. Like the beach at dawn. Like a prom.

"This is so nice," I told Gary.

"What?"

"This, that, everything," I said, as another weird week came to a close.

As the boy drove us home, "Tiny Dancer" played on the radio, a song that always comes on at just the right time, usually at dusk, like the feel-good soundtrack of a Cameron Crowe movie.

"Best song ever," I shouted to my son. "Isn't this the best song ever?"

I told him how we screamed it back in college — sang it in all-caps — and how we're all still screaming it today, 125 years later.

"Sure Dad," my son said with a shrug, but soon he was howling it too, we both were.

"HOLD ME CLOSER, TINY DANCER ... COUNT THE HEAD-LIGHTS ON THE HIGHWAY..."

Like a tree full of birds.

slaw saved My Parents

I am a pastoral man surrounded by cement. I also like pastrami a lot, so I guess I am stuck in this hot, over-paved city forever.

My new memoir will be titled "Brined Meats and Me." All I've got so far is the title. But that's the most important part. If you have a great bride, you don't really need a great wedding. Book titles are the same way.

Speaking of weddings, the lovely and patient older daughter is going to have one. From all indications, she's pretty into it. As of today, she's bought two wedding dresses — she can't make up her mind — and may be out shopping for a third.

"As long as you don't have two grooms," I told her.

It's been an agonizing wait for her and her fiancé, Finn. First, the wedding was to be in April, then June. Now, it's pushed back till next summer.

But, by gawd, she glows.

Sure, the delays hurt, yet they are hanging in, as are many couples in this summer of lost weddings.

Nothing is lost though. Only postponed as anticipation continues to build. So much of life is anticipation. Just like so much of life is good pastrami.

At Langer's Deli in Los Angeles, they serve the best pastrami the world has ever known, topped by a roof of slaw, cuddled by soft, warm rye with a snappy crust.

I was telling the kids the other night how important coleslaw was to my family growing up. Essentially, it saved my parents' marriage.

It was a somewhat rocky marriage, as many marriages are — "Knott's Landing," only louder. I'm fairly sure my father would've bolted, except that my mother had that French twinkle about her and wore heels when she vacuumed.

But most of all, she made the best coleslaw you've ever tasted, a silky, finely grated slaw with red onions, vinegar, mayo.

My dad was a slave to that slaw. They would have it on Saturday nights with barbecued ribs. Like most men, Dad never felt food on his face, and the sauce would get everywhere, a smeary war paint, while we all ate ribs and watched Lawrence Welk on TV.

Mom loved Lawrence Welk, and Dad despised him; that's just how everything went. Even a schmaltzy German band leader could set them off.

"Anna-one, anna-two, anna-treeeeee ..."

They'd have split, if not for that slaw, the ribs, the garlic bread, all the culinary glues that saved their marriage and thereby, probably my childhood (though I always suspected that Mom could've had many husbands — a harem of husbands — and might've one day ended up with one she liked).

Life can be such a series of close calls, can't it?

Anyway, I'm still impressed by the sheer power of slaw. The boy and I made slaw together the other day, and I was telling him about the restorative power of his grandma's recipe, which we were recreating, elbow to elbow.

My son was slicing some onions, and I was grating-grating-grating the cabbage by hand, the only way to ensure its feathery texture.

We fell into a rhythm, the boy and I, with him chopping the red onion in tandem with the pace of my grating, a sort of father-son bossa nova.

In about 30 seconds, I realized he was mocking me. When I stopped, he stopped. When I started, he started. Such a goof. My dad would've loved him.

You know, life happens in kitchens, more than bedrooms, more than dens.

Increasingly, fathers are doing much of the cooking, a good example for sons, an even better example for daughters.

Because when you're out shopping for a boyfriend or a husband — they're also available online now — it's nice to find a candidate who shares life's little obligations.

Finn, the fiancé, gladly shares the chores, which is what makes me feel so good about my daughter's pending marriage.

In fact, last month, as the wedding was being postponed a second time, the lovely older daughter burst into happy tears over the way Finn carefully plated a homecooked meal in a way that pleased her.

It was just a small and tender kindness, but she's a wise woman — her mother's daughter — and she realizes the value of small and tender kindnesses.

And in that moment, in that small kindness, she knew she'd found her guy.

Father's Daze

I was having a little pity party the other day — a cranky mood triggered by some rancid cut-rate coffee and the thought of swapping out my cable system, which I have to do myself, with COVID safeguards in place.

I mean, I get it. Who wants a repair person in their home these days? And what sort of repair person wants to go into multiple dens to tug cables just so Aunt Flo can watch that pistol Kelly Ripa?

Still, the thought of self-installing the modem/router/cable box/ Apple TV device and making it all sync up in multiple rooms was fouling my mood. Could take years.

Seriously, I'd rather play catch with a porcupine.

My son picked up on my crankiness, of course, and teased me about it, the way good roommates do. And when the teasing subsided, he was a little extra goofy — which is *really* goofy — in an effort to cheer me up.

When the wolf/dog tongue-kissed him ferociously, he tongue-kissed her right back. That sort of thing.

Worked well enough. I perked back up, made him pizza for dinner, then watched "Seinfeld" and "Friday Night Lights" with him, two old shows we're hooked on.

In an Olympics of great TV dads, Kyle Chandler wins the gold medal for his work in "Friday Night Lights." He was like a great character in literature, strong but flawed, undeniably capable yet second-guessed every step of the journey.

There is a recipe for good television: Strong dads are in charge of difficult situations — locker rooms, or Italian mobs — then second-guessed in their own homes.

I find that authentic and entertaining. In Chandler's case, he could work all day with ornery linebackers and chirpy running backs. But he couldn't win an argument with his 15-year-old daughter.

Show of hands: Does that feel real?

Well, it does to my son and me. Family dynamics are among the most interesting dynamics, the most complicated and challenging, relentlessly rich.

One day, I would love to do a TV show, a book or a rock opera as resonant and wonderful as "Friday Night Lights."

"Like family," I told my son as we watched last night.

"Huh?"

"Good TV characters become family," I say.

Speaking of family, I was talking to a young friend the other day, and she wasn't sure whether she and her husband would have children.

Millennials like them seem to want to make their own way. They are less inclined to buy into the standard American dream, of a house, a couple of kids, a golden retriever, a kitten, hamsters, snakes, turtles, mice, a mortgage, life insurance, car insurance, index funds, long-term warranties, measles, mumps, deductibles, property taxes, roof repairs, termites, monthly cable fees, car payments, etc.

I mean, who wouldn't crave all that?

Truthfully, a family can get out of hand very quickly, and soon you're feeding every mouth on the planet, and you never have a moment to yourself because you're always working, repairing, cooking, cleaning, coaching, or running to the pet store for more kibble.

It's a hectic life, but what else you gonna do, take up bowling?

I've liked being a dad. I find it profound and relentlessly rich. Even kind of fun.

I like the way sons and daughters hang off your shoulder when you're reading the box scores. I like the way they'll just suddenly wrestle you to the ground for no reason.

And occasionally, when you're in a little funk, your kids will lift you up. Not always, but often enough. They'll sit in your lap and act extra goofy. They'll make you smile the way only kids can.

Indeed, sometimes our children are more than noisy obligations. Sometimes, they are our saviors.

Happy Father's Day.

summer
of Love

Summer is coming whether you like it or not, so you'd better like it.

It'll be a summer without baseball or weddings or reunions. It'll be a remarkable summer, just the same.

All summers are remarkable in some way — might be the way you lather up the sweet corn, then sear it on the grill. Might be the way the baked beans slide a little bit into the bun.

Might be a run on the beach at dawn, no one around but the porpoise and the snowy plover. Might be the summer you read the best book you've ever read, or fall for the checker at the supermarket, the one with a nose ring.

You just never know with summer.

This will, no doubt, be a fractured summer — you could put it in a sling and a cast. What of summer's grand traditions: movies, first dates, beer gardens and fireworks? No one knows.

A friendly side note to Major League Baseball: Play ball, you morons, or risk losing the respect and affection of the nation.

For four months, I have been walking by dormant Little League fields, sad and silent. Eight-year-olds play for free. You can play for 70% in a country with runaway unemployment and a struggling underclass. Not only are the 8-year-olds missing a season, the cities have padlocked the fields.

Basically, they've sent summer up the river.

But the MLB has a chance to rescue summer, to bring back its edgy opera, to make America roar again.

Highly paid men on both sides risk losing the moment in petty battles over percentages (honestly, boys, look up from your lobster bisque just once).

Hey, baseball, America turns its lonely eyes to you. Coo, coo, ca-choo.

I say that because I like to use the phrase "coo, coo, ca-choo" whenever possible. I work it into daily conversation, toasts, tantrums, evening prayers.

It is still the greatest song lyric ever, nonsensical yet playfully droll ... just perfect.

In fact, place movies like "The Graduate" among your fractured summer pleasures, though there is no movie quite like "The Graduate," just as there is no player quite like DiMaggio.

Though it premiered at Christmas (1967), "The Graduate" remains the quintessential summer movie, smeared in tanning oil and sporting a golfer's glow, not to mention a sun-kissed Anne Bancroft, the first (and best) MILF.

Talk about glow. Bancroft shouldn't have won the Oscar for that role, she should've won three.

By the way, I read last week that much of the dialogue for "The Graduate" comes directly from the book, which was written in the poolside bar of what is now the Langham Hotel in Pasadena.

A poolside bar? At the magnificent old Langham?

True. Charles Webb wrote that brilliant book in a pool haze of tequila and Coppertone. So maybe there's hope for me. Maybe, I'll have a literary career after all.

Waiter!!!

Listen, I could build one hell of a bar tab at the Langham and never get a word written. I'd call my buddies Bittner and Big-Wave Dave:

"Hey, get over here!"

"Why?"

"I'm writing a bestseller. Bring your suit."

Three months later, there'd still be nothing on the page except sun screen and cocktail sauce.

Writers don't need friends, they need neuroses, which is why California doesn't really produce all that many good writers. Too much sunshine. Too many juicy tidbits.

At least that's my excuse.

Coo, coo, ca-choo ...

White Fang's Dad

'm walking the wolf at dusk — the hot sun is soft now, as if apologizing.

This is a perfect evening to walk a wolf, except she can't seem to get out of first gear, sniffling, watering, nudging the landscape with her nose, every dandelion, every daisy.

"Come on," I say. "Will ya come on?"

The wolf won't acknowledge me, but she comes along just the same, in the lingering twilight of a long June day.

From my estimate, the wolf knows about 40 words, including two Yiddish expressions — putz and kishka — and one Russian drinking song.

The defiant wolf doesn't respond to any of them. She knows them and ignores them.

Yet I appreciate her cool indifference, her icy Grace Kelly visage. The wolf is a magnificent creature, no question, and like so many beauties, she knows it.

On our walks, infatuated strangers bring her treats. They are more likely to know her name than mine.

"White Fang!" they say. "How ya you doin' there, White Fang?"

As with a high-achieving child — a shortstop, a violinist — I am best known as "White Fang's dad."

I figure one day she will be "discovered," like Lana Turner at the malt shop. White Fang will probably be calmly licking bourbon from my ankle at a bus stop on Hollywood Boulevard, and some producer will spot her big-screen potential and want to build a summer movie franchise around her.

"Has she ever acted?" the producer will ask.

"Every day of her life," I'll say.

That kind of stuff still happens out here. The right putz turns a corner. Boom, you're a star.

Look, I am at the mercy of so many forces — appetites, impulses, thirsts and instincts. Now, I am at the mercy of this ridiculous wolf-dog, a Siberian immigrant.

I'm not even sure she's "legal," in the cruel lingo of immigration. My late son showed up with this blue-eyed pup one day, and now she is his surrogate, carrying on the legacy of a young man who left too soon, with too many smiles still in the tank.

Like him, the furry Russian makes us smile. And that is enough.

Not that she's perfect or anything. With the summery weather, her coat flies off like bales of cotton. It's more than molting. It's like a low-pressure system of fur, right out of Canada.

But she does make us smile.

We feed her bison now, that's how spoiled she's become. The bison comes in fat tubes, like liver sausage. The label says it also contains cranberries and blueberries. The bison loaf was Dogpark Gary's retirement gift to me and White Fang.

Like I said, random admirers bring her gifts.

In a few weeks, the boy and I are considering taking this silly creature, this blizzard of fur, on a mid-summer road trip to Chicago, across Zion and the Rockies, into the mosquito belt of the sultry Midwest.

"Wait'll you see Dubuque," I was telling the dog the other day.

The Mississippi will be our Rhine, and we'll take a day to explore the river towns: Keokuk, McGregor, Le Claire, in search of prairie poets and little cafes where they still play John Prine.

I can romanticize anything, true, but I can't quite do those river towns justice. I need their trademark sonics now — the slamming of screen doors and the snoring of trucks as they downshift coming into town.

The boy and I will order giant ice cream cones that will melt too quickly and sit on park benches next to lilac trees. We'll watch the way old men in overalls slowly unfold from their pickup trucks, as if setting up a church chair.

After the fireflies come out, we'll go to dinner.

The boy and I will wrap our summer in this road trip to the Upper Midwest. In many ways, it'll be a cultural revelation for the boy, who's never driven further than Phoenix.

So it'll be a good time for some lazy adventure, in the spirit of Tom and Huck, Thelma and Louise, Bonnie and Clyde.

Make way for us, America. Set aside a room or two.

In a few weeks, we're coming home.

Florida Is where we Met

When I hear people are heading to Florida, I think, "Order the broiled flounder and get out," because that's pretty much the highlight of any visit. Or stepping on a sting ray. Or opening a kitchen cabinet and hearing the water bugs scatter. Florida is not for wimps. In many ways, it is our last wilderness.

And a freak show in the first degree.

There are stretches of mangrove that will never be tamed. They've nearly butchered the Everglades, that's true, yet there are vast stretches of coastline and swampland that defy development.

In Florida, hurricanes are the only law enforcement. Every few years, a new one comes along and sweeps away some coastal community, knocks down the replanted palms, bashes the jalousie windows, and Florida starts from scratch again, herds of alligators watching and laughing.

I've been thinking of Florida lately, as people bag on it over how it's handled COVID.

Oddly, I have the urge to return. Posh had family there. Florida is where we met, and to seduce her way back then, I bought a ragtop jeep and used to take her flying across some local dunes near Fort Lauderdale. It was like trying to break a bronco — the jeep, not Posh. But there were similarities there too.

I lived there a couple of years long enough to realize that Florida is a cheesy game show, with striking scenery and the most beautiful women in the world, one of whom I married.

So good things happen in Florida too.

I'm thinking now I'd like to drive the entire perimeter, from Pensacola down the West Coast, to the Keys, then back up the East Coast to Rickey's Tavern in Hollywood, where they used to serve steamed clams for about a dime.

When I was 21 and dating the most beautiful girl in the state, it was about all I could afford. And it was enough.

Oh Florida. Like a lot of places, like a lot of people, maybe it needs a second chance.

I Love Millennials

Semi-retirement suits me. I've been reading hungrily, in a way I haven't since college, and the other day, I cleaned the oven for the first time in 15 years.

Cleaning an oven is a nasty business, and I didn't mind it one bit. The results are dramatic, and you can point to the task for weeks later, and say, "Look at that gleaming oven. I barely recognize it, do you?"

Not so much with writing or reading. They both seem indulgent to me, when really they are important to my spirit and my financial well-being. It's just harder to quantify.

And I love it all so much, I have trouble thinking of them — writing and reading — as tasks. It's like getting paid to love Angie Dickinson, or baseball, or Brahms, which I do inherently.

So I spend my days buying books or thinking of ordering books or jotting down titles of books I long to read. I poke my nose in those neighborhood book hutches, looking for treasures. "Ah, look, a Michael Connelly!"

The authors are all over the map: Kooser. Fitzgerald. Taddeo. I don't care the status of the writer, only that he or she tells a great truth here and there. That he or she cleans my oven.

Got a book tip? Please share. The way I used to look forward to new record albums, that's the way I now look forward to new books.

You remember that don't you, the anticipation of tearing the shrink wrap off a new album, running your thumbnail across the crease, like releasing it from jail?

Then you'd take that new vinyl disc, free of fingerprints and dust, and add your own, inadvertently, no matter how careful you were.

Drop the needle and your bedroom would bulge with the Moody Blues or Emerson, Lake & Palmer. Tull! A new album was like a holiday.

Who needed parents in that moment? Who needs them now? I mean, really.

In 1968, the world was ending, just as it is now, and the music was amazing and everything seemed more thoughtful and creative and candid. Our parents' world was under attack, just like now, except now, there is a groundswell always on social media that I often think doesn't represent America as a whole. Or does it?

Maybe social media is today's rock n' roll, though I don't find it very artful. It is rock n' roll only in the sense that it conveys an energy and a passion.

Social media sure follows the American tradition of not recognizing the quietest among us, the ones who silently go about their work, take care of others, and are distrustful of the loudest lout at the party.

If nothing else, we live in very interesting times.

Look, I'm just a wayward French existentialist hobo, a writer of soft suburban sonnets. I mean, what do I know? Even Jesus had more money than I do.

But I think the irony of ironies — the triple-scoop cone of ironies — is that most of the millennials I know are thoughtful and idealistic, like their parents were in 1968. Big whiners too, like their parents. I find that all sorts of fascinating. We get the children we deserve.

As with all groups, boomers and millennials are more alike than different. Both were stir-crazy over normal conventions. Both were rabid thinkers, with a self-righteous verve. Both called for sweeping and dramatic change.

Boomers gave the world great music. They also invented cell-phones and expanded the internet, two tools the millennials want to use to murder us.

Love you millennials. Love you not. I don't have much fondness for your so-called "cancel culture," where you shut down the things you disagree with. That's not so far from what Stalin, Mao and Joseph McCarthy used to do.

But I mostly love the millennials, the idealism, the passion. I hope you have more follow-through than your predecessors. I hope the rigors of the workaday world don't bleed the idealism right out of you.

I also hope that, in preaching tolerance, you show a little once in a while.

Forgive Us our Gin

I like the clink of two martini glasses, the ping of the rims, the night's first kiss.

I like when they backlight the bottles behind the bar, so you can see the bits of orange in the Grand Marnier and the pumpkin-blush of the Scotch, like it's in love or something.

I like cocktail napkins on the bar top, in little plastic boxes provided by Seagram's.

I like the banter of bartenders and the way beautiful women shimmy aboard a too-high stool.

So glad the bars are coming back.

I write a lot about booze, no question, and I am always careful to suggest moderation. Seriously, I need you around. I mean, who else would ever hang out with me? Vagrants? Judges? Bookies?

So we should drink to drink another day. We should always drink so we can toast another Christmas season and the madness that ensues.

Speaking of madness, I'm considering a podcast: "Drinks with Idiots," where we bring in sportswriters and other misfits to share their favorite bar stories and drinking tips.

It's not lost on me that one of the great male dreams used to be opening a cool bar. Now it's starting a cool podcast.

Lord, help us all ...

Society started going downhill when they starting putting ketchup in little plastic packets. And when TV quit being free. And *Playboy* went full frontal.

And when podcasts became bars.

Anyway, I check the gin twice a day, the way other guys check the stock market. I check the level of the gin to be sure it's not evaporating and to be sure we have enough for later in the day, when I might need a sip or two to make sense of the world.

Not always, not every day. But once in a while, in any icy glass with a wicked wreath of lime and a splash of tonic — not too much. I want to taste the juniper tree. I want to bite the bark. A good drink is visceral like that.

In last night's gin and tonic, the two slices of lime were all over each other, like kids at a drive-in. Honestly, I found it kind of romantic.

These are all topics we'll talk about on my new podcast, as well as who was the better manager, Earl Weaver or Sparky Anderson, and other major issues of the day. Baryshnikov or Nureyev? Redford of Newman? Zeppelin or the Stones?

We'll talk about how our dads influenced us — like no man before or since — and women own us, even our daughters.

In every podcast, we will keep a top-10 ranking, subject to change, on key elements to a well-balanced life.

The Inaugural List of Things We Need:

- A dog
- A best friend
- A favorite author
- A favorite band
- A dive bar that makes you happy
- The ocean, a lake or a small stream
- Family
- Exercise
- Faith (in something ... anything)
- Laughter

That's my list. What's yours?

You may note that family is No. 7. Hope no one takes that personally.

Besides, laughter is No. 10, when it should be No. 1.

Look, doesn't matter the rank. Rank isn't important here. As a nation, we spend far too much time fighting over who's No. 1, rather than celebrating good stuff in general.

I'll confess something right here: I can easily go a day without drink, but not without music or a little something juicy to read.

I can go two days without friendship, but only two.

Obviously, it's not easy being me. I wander Los Angeles like a mad Danish prince in flip-flops, missing spots when I shave, and putting groceries in the wrong shopping cart.

"Whoops. Sorry ..."

I have no head for business, no nose for numbers. My body looks like an ear of corn.

Almost every week, I do the same things, wash the same seven t-shirts, eat the same seven meals, jog the same seven miles. I probably listen to too much James Taylor.

There is so much sameness. But it's a sweet and reassuring sameness.

My buddy Langley passed along something the other day: "I hate when it's dark and my brain is like, 'Hey, you know what we haven't thought of in a while? Monsters.'"

Point is, many of us are hard-wired toward gloom. It can take a conscious effort to see the anti-gloom.

So I call a pal, play a prank, dial up a song from the '70s I've heard a gazillion times — a relic, a reference point, a lighthouse for the soul.

And I sip a little gin.

Here comes The Bride

The bride arrived at church in a vintage white Rolls, on sea breezes, just ahead of the summer solstice.

My older daughter had been imagining this day her entire life. She pictured beaming crowds, old friends, lightning bursts of laughter.

She imagined flower girls somersaulting in charmeuse petticoats. She imagined chatty and gallant ushers.

On this day, there was none of that.

But sometimes, less is more. The tiny ceremony was personal and poignant, attended only by me, her sister and her sister's boyfriend, her brother, and the man who owns her heart.

In hindsight, maybe no wedding needs to be bigger than that.

Large weddings are wonderful, but they can easily become like Renaissance fairs. Something borrowed, something blue, butterflies, Vivaldi, trumpets, horses, swans, gossip, flop sweat, cummerbunds, contract law, romance, heroines, harps.

This wedding was stripped of most of the usual excess — the filigree, the flourishes. But it was far from austere. Her dress? Magnificent. The altar? Heavenly.

Just to hear Pachelbel wash across the church again stirred the soul.

Of course, the bride really needed her mother there, to lick her fingers and smooth her daughter's hair. To fluff the bridal veil. To scold her daughter not to cry: "You'll melt your makeup," her mother would say, even as she cried herself.

Instead, she had her sister, who did outstanding work as a surrogate mom and solo bridesmaid.

And her dad, of course. Lots of luck with that.

"Show up, shut up and pay up," was the advice from a friend. So I mostly did.

For the record, it's hard to hug a bride, the dress so billowy. You lean in carefully, watching where you step ... oops.

Hugging a bride is like hugging a snowstorm, and in the limo ride over, or in helping her from the car, I kept snagging things and stepping on the train, or whatever they call the parts of the dress that surround her like gallons of meringue.

There really should be tutorials on how a father should hug the bride. Maybe I'll make one. Till then, just do the best you can.

With trembling fingers, I helped my son pin his boutonniere, then smoothed the shoulders of his jacket and heartily slapped him on the back.

BAM!

It was the kind of pre-game backslap that wobbly, overdressed men often perform at formal occasions.

BAM! BAM! BAM! "Go get 'em!"

As the 3 p.m. ceremony approached, other family members — cousins, sisters, uncles, aunts — tuned into the video feed. In Chicago, they sipped and yelped. In New York, they even made a cake.

When the ceremony was done, the groom danced a little jig. We all did. In celebration. In relief.

As with a lot of couples, their wedding date kept getting pushed by COVID, and they finally decided: Let's just do it.

Rather than wait another year, they'd tie the knot in a micro-wedding in magnificent St. Monica's Church, then celebrate with all their friends and family at a later date, with a reenactment and reception.

Whatever happens a year from now, this will be tough to top.

It was a full weekend, with a bawdy rehearsal dinner and anticipatory toasts, texts and phone calls.

On Friday night, we ate up all the sushi in Los Angeles — there is no sushi left, don't even try.

Finn, the fiancé, likes a feast where plates fill the table, edge to edge, lip to lip. He ordered everything on the menu, and several things (I suspect) from the joint across the street.

We ate every part of the sea: monkfish liver, gizzard shad. The prawns came to the table with their antenna still spinning.

Ewwwww! Bravo! I felt like Morey Amsterdam at a state dinner.

"Could I get some ketchup?" I asked the waitress.

"No," she said.

For three hours, all we did was laugh and drink and nosh.

Honestly, could Saturday get any better?

The wedding day started early. Makeup took two hours for a bride who doesn't really need any. My older daughter has a natural amber, a combo of my Irish blush and a smokey satin from her mama's Sicilian side.

Against the sleigh-ride white of her wedding dress, she looked like the Fourth of July.

"Babe of a bride!" her little sister beamed. "Babe of a bride!"

Flowers arrived, then the limo, which glided up Lincoln Boulevard like a giant swan. I'm in the backseat with the bride, and all I can think is: What's going on here? This isn't the sort of daughter you ever "give away." Get a grip, man!

The day was delicate, sort of silky — not too cool, not too warm. Good for photos. Good for waiting around outside, kicking at the sidewalk, as weddings always require.

Of all the customs — baptisms, confirmations, graduations — a wedding is the most deliberate. It's a bet that love can outlast the extended warranty. It's a wager in the right direction.

d marriage means the bed will always be warm on winter nights. That your birthday will always have a cake and candles. That someone will be around to help doctor the soup.

In the future, I might attend weddings the way Leopold Bloom attended the funerals of complete strangers ... as a public show of support. I'll show up to honor random couples the way I support bookstores and bassoon recitals.

Look, lately, the world seems locked in utter turmoil. The bad news piles up every hour — when will it stop? The other day, some idiots were actually talking about tearing down Mount Rushmore. And the Loch Ness monster was "trending."

For the love of God ...

Yet, on a gauzy June day, the sirens stopped a moment. My beautiful daughter took a man's hand and vowed, "No way. No way can this stop us."

I think I heard her late mother weeping. And my heart ripping at the seams.

"Do you take this woman ...?" the monsignor asked.

"I do," the groom responded.

Oh baby. Bravo.

More Books
by Chris Erskine

Man of the House

Daditude

Surviving Suburbia

About the Author

Chris Erskine has been chronicling life in Los Angeles for more than 30 years. As a staffer for the *Los Angeles Times*, he wrote about sports, travel, entertainment and lifestyle sections. Best known for his regular columns about suburban family life, he is the author of three books of essays: *Surviving Suburbia*, *Man of the House* and *Daditude*.

The Chicago native has also worked for papers in Miami and New Orleans. He is aggressive in all pursuits, yet successful in few and consciously makes a point of remembering only the past 48 hours of his life. The only things he trusts are church ladies, children and dogs — and he's not so sure about the church ladies. He once scored 5 points against the Harlem Globetrotters, all in the first half. In the second half, they pants'ed him.

For more about Chris Erskine and his writings please see Chris-ErskineLA.com.

About The Sager Group

The Sager Group was founded in 1984. In 2012, it was chartered as a multimedia content brand, with the intention of empowering those who create art—an umbrella beneath which makers can pursue, and profit from, their craft directly, without gatekeepers. TSG publishes books; ministers to artists and provides modest grants; designs logos, products and packaging, and produces documentary, feature, and commercial films. By harnessing the means of production, The Sager Group helps artists help themselves. For more information, visit TheSagerGroup.net

More Books
From The Sager Group

Mandela was Late: Odd Things & Essays From the Seinfeld Writer Who Coined Yada, Yada and Made Spongeworthy a Compliment by Peter Mehlman

#MeAsWell, A Novel by Peter Mehlman

The Orphan's Daughter, A Novel by Jan Cherubin

Words to Repair the World: Stories of Life, Humor and Everyday Miracles by Mike Levine

Miss Havilland, A Novel by Gay Daly

High Tolerance, A Novel by Mike Sager

Lifeboat No. 8: Surviving the Titanic by Elizabeth Kaye

See our entire library at TheSagerGroup.net

THE SAGER GROUP

Artifex Te Adiuva